Being Sent:

Jonah's mission,

God's mission,

Our mission

Tim Carter

GILEAD
B O O K S
PUBLISHING

Gilead Books Publishing
Corner Farm
West Knapton
Malton
North Yorkshire YO17 8JB UK
www.GileadBooksPublishing.com

First published in Great Britain, October 2014

2 4 6 8 10 9 7 5 3 1

British Library Cataloguing-in-Publication Data:

A catalogue record for this book is available from the British Library.

ISBN: 978-0-9926713-5-8

The publisher makes every effort to ensure that the papers used in our books are made from trees that have been legally sourced from well-managed and credibly certified forests by using a printer awarded FSC & PEFC chain of custody certification.

Cover design: Nathan Ward

Editor: David Burton

Contents

Acknowledgements

Thanks are due to:

The Home Groups at All Saints and elsewhere who welcomed me and reflected with me on the story of Jonah.

Liz, my wife, for her love, patience, and encouragement.

Tabitha and Nathaniel for putting up with a grumpy daddy when I got stuck.

Introduction

In the summer of 2011 my family and I moved to Priorslee, a recently built suburb of Telford, to begin a Pioneer Ministry.[1] I had worked as a curate in a traditional parish, but had been encouraged within that to explore and develop new initiatives to reach out to those in the community who did not connect easily with the church. My experience of doing this had further convinced me that the church needs to continue finding fresh ways of expressing its faith if it is to reach out effectively to the growing numbers of people in our communities who have had little or no contact with the church or with Christians. Our sense

[1] Pioneer Ministry is a recognised ministry in the Church of England particularly focused on growing and nurturing new church communities and fresh expressions on church.

of call to Telford was founded on this general conviction, and on a belief that God was calling us to explore this form of ministry in the specific context of Priorslee, in order to reach the people here with the good news of Jesus.

Fairly early in our time here we began holding monthly prayer meetings focussed on the people who live and work in our community, seeking to discern what God was calling us to do, and how we were to do it. At one of the first meetings we used the book of Jonah to provide a framework for our reflection and prayers, and this proved to be a very fruitful exercise.

It was so fruitful that when I was invited to visit some of the small groups at one of our supporting churches, All Saints in Wellington, I decided to use some of our time together to read Jonah and to reflect on what it has to say to us about mission. We read the whole of the book out loud, with different people taking different parts. Some groups were more energetic in their role-playing of the sailors' efforts to get to land - and the vomiting fish - than others were, but all of the groups found new perspectives on the story as they gave voices to the different characters. This book is based on the reflections that came from those groups, supplemented by further thought and reading on my part.

In some senses this is not a finished work. We are still in the early days of our church-planting, and that means that few of the stories that I will share have endings. These reflections are works in progress, and are subject to being changed by the way that things work out in practice. I could have waited to share this more widely until I had more stories, more definite answers, and more evidence for my hunches and assertions. I haven't, because I wanted to share something from the early days of this kind of endeavour, with all the uncertainty that comes along with it. I felt that it would be helpful to get something out there, not just as the first chapters of a book about the success of a church plant, but as the whole of the story to date, before we can speak with the benefit of hindsight.

My hope is that this book can be part of a conversation in your church, small group, or church-planting team. You might read it together in your small group, maybe as part of a Lent or Advent course. I hope that you will disagree with me in places, and be able to explore why you disagree. I also hope that there will be "Aha" moments, when you will find a phrase or sentence that captures something that has been stirring in your spirit but that you have not been able to express to your own satisfaction. Most of all I hope that engaging with this story will build you up and encourage you in the mission that God has called you to.

Each chapter focuses on a different character or set of characters in the book of Jonah, sharing some reflections on mission that were sparked in our minds as we considered them. Within the chapters, each section ends with some questions, many of which are still live questions for us. They are there for you to ponder and discuss. I don't have the answers to all of them, and I could not have the answers to many of them, as those answers will be specific to your situation.

I suspect that it's quite unusual for the introduction of a book to suggest that the reader should put the book down and go and read another one before continuing, but that is what is going to happen now. Because we dive straight into the middle of the story, I believe that you will get more out of this book if you put it down now, go and get a Bible, and read the book of Jonah at least twice. As you do, ask God to speak to you, and be ready to listen. Write down what strikes you, think about which of the characters you identify with, and why. Then come back to this book and join the conversation.

Chapter 1

The Sailors

Prayer, Actions, and Faith

Then the mariners were afraid, and each cried to his god. They threw the cargo that was in the ship into the sea, to lighten it for them. (Jonah 1:5)

When we first meet the sailors they are in the middle of a crisis. They fear for their lives, and are focussing all their energies on what they need to do in order to survive. This is not a place for contemplation or theological debate. What they need is an urgent solution to a life-threatening catastrophe. In this maelstrom, we find them doing two things. They are praying, and they are working.

On the face of it, this approach seems to be a fine example of the oft-quoted maxim, "Pray as though everything depends on God, and work as though everything depends on you."[2] However, a close look at the development of the story, and at the way their prayers change as the story unfolds, raises important questions about this way of thinking.

The sailors are straining every sinew, doing all that they can, not resting for a moment. They're working but it's not working. The ship is still foundering. They are crying out to their gods, praying, assaulting the gates of heaven. They're praying but it's not working. The ship is still foundering. So the captain approaches the slightly odd passenger, the one who is comatose through the storm. The captain instructs him to call on his god. This seems to cast some doubt on the faith that the sailors have in the prayers they have made to their own gods.

Next they cast lots to see who is responsible for the storm. They give any god who might be interested the

[2] Variously and vaguely accredited to Augustine, Ignatius Loyola and others, though rarely with a precise reference. For a fuller discussion see http://www.shalem.org/index.php/resources/newsletter/newsletter-archive/winter01#04

opportunity to speak into the situation, in the best way that they know. The outcome of what they hear is Jonah's instruction for them to throw him into the sea. They don't want to hear this. They know that their own gods take a dim view of murder, and are fairly sure that Jonah's God, the Lord, is likely to share that view. So they work. They row as hard as they can for the shore. The sailors are straining every sinew, doing all that they can, not resting for a moment. They're working but it's not working. The ship is still foundering.

Exhausted by their own efforts, finally the sailors pray to the Lord, and follow Jonah's instructions. They pray for the Lord's forgiveness, and, trusting that the prayer has been heard, do something in line with the prayer: they throw Jonah into the sea. The sea is calmed and the sailors are convinced of the reality of the power of the Lord God, convinced enough to make sacrifices and vows to God.

When we meet the sailors they are praying, but what they are doing reveals that they don't believe that their prayers will be answered. Their search for another god to pray to further reveals this lack of faith. The contrast between this and their final prayer, and their matching action, reinforces the impression that their initial prayers lacked faith.

In three of the accounts of Jesus' life we are told of an episode in which another boat with a sleeping passenger, on a different sea, gets caught in a storm.[3] Jesus and his followers are crossing Lake Galilee in a fishing boat, when the weather rapidly worsens, and the disciples start to fear for their safety. They wake Jesus and say, "Lord, save us! We are perishing." In response Jesus does two things. He calms the storm and asks his friends why they are afraid - where their faith is. This might seem a little harsh, especially in the light of what we've just been saying about Jonah's fellow travellers. At least the disciples weren't trying to row to shore, or rescue themselves with their own strength and seamanship. They weren't praying one way and acting another. They went to Jesus, and prayed to him, "save us". Nevertheless, it seems that they didn't actually believe that Jesus was going to be able to do anything about it.

This lack of belief is shown in two things. The first is Jesus' witness that they are afraid. If you truly believe

---

[3] Matthew 8:23-27, Mark 4:35-41, Luke 8:22-25

that you are safe, then you do not fear. If you fear, then it reveals that you do not believe that you are safe. The second is their amazement at what Jesus does: at the calming of the storm. If they had been expecting Jesus to save them, they would not have been amazed when he did. Their amazement reveals their lack of expectation, their lack of faith.

Towards the end of the book of Acts[4] there is another story about some sailors in a storm that might also guide our thinking about prayer. Paul, under armed guard, is on his way to Rome to stand trial before the Emperor. It is late in the season for making this journey, and the sailors are pushing their luck by attempting to complete the voyage before the winter storms set in. Their gamble fails, and they are caught in a ferocious Mediterranean gale.

In contrast with Jonah's sailors, who pray and work, and with Jesus' sailors who only pray, these sailors do not pray, but work to try and survive the storm. They throw their cargo overboard, they throw ropes round the hull of the ship to reinforce it against the battering waves, they even throw the ship's tackle overboard.

[4] Acts 27:13-44

But there is no hint that anybody is praying. Anyone, that is, except Paul. He has been praying, but the most important feature of his prayer is not what he said, but what he heard. He has received God's assurance that all will be well, and he instructs his fellow travellers in what to do. Most tellingly, he persuades them to do it. Paul listens to God, and believes what he is told. He tells the others what he has heard, and they believe him. Faith leads to faith. As the storm continues to rage, Paul's persuasiveness and the actions of the sailors continue to demonstrate faith.

Paul gets the ship's company to eat, and then to throw the remaining grain overboard. They will need strength for the swim to the beach, and God has placed the resources they need to hand. They are to make use of them, and then lighten the load by discarding the remainder. That they do this shows that they believe Paul's prophecy. They believe that the boat will be lost, so there is no point trying to preserve the valuable cargo. They believe that they will survive, so they don't attempt to conserve the food that they will not need when they are on the beach.

Paul's example of faith inspires the leader of the

soldiers guarding him, who now takes responsibility for directing the abandonment of the ship. He prevents the soldiers from killing the prisoners, and orders everybody to jump overboard, some to swim and some to be washed shorewards clinging to the debris of the disintegrating ship. These are the actions of people who have reached the end of their own resources and are entrusting themselves to the mercy of God as promised by God's messenger.

In these three stories we see different combinations of prayer and action, combinations which say something about the faith of the people praying, and which raise questions for us about our own prayers and faith. We see that when we are faced with a storm, depending on our own strength is not going to see us safely to harbour. We also see that faithless prayers are not the answer either, but that instead we need to cultivate a faith that says no to fear.[5]

This is not to deny that we get afraid. Neither is it to make us feel guilty when we are afraid. But it should

[5] I love Dave Godfrey's setting of the storm on Galilee story to music, "I know" from the album, "Zoom", from which I've borrowed this phrase.

encourage us to acknowledge the fear that a situation causes us, and then look beyond the immediate situation to the eternal promises of God, and to choose to act in the greater reality of those promises.

To ponder:

As we live out God's call on our lives, and particularly in the storms, what place do we give to work and to prayer?

Do we ever evade our responsibility to take faithful action because we have prayed about a situation?

Are we more likely to work as though it all depends on us, revealing a lack of concrete trust in God?

How can we develop a healthy and trusting outlook that enables us to pray with deep faith and to play our part (rather than attempting to play God's) in the answers to those prayers?

God is always there first

Then they cried out to the Lord, 'Please, O Lord, we pray, do not let us perish on account of this man's life. Do not make us guilty of innocent blood; for you, O Lord, have done as it pleased you.' (Jonah 1:14)

As we have already seen in the prayer life of these sailors, it is obvious from this story that they are not blank slates as far as religious belief and expression is concerned. There are two aspects of this that are particularly important when it comes to mission. Firstly, their religious belief that there is something other than the material world. Secondly, their moral sense of right and wrong.

It is most likely that the sailors would have had a syncretic religion - a worldview containing many gods. A god for the home, and another for the marketplace. A god for the sea, and another for the land. A god for each nation, and a family god for each hearth. This worldview would have left them open to the suggestion that there is another god, who they hadn't heard of before, who was acting to cause this storm, and who might demand something of them. It probably would have made them resistant to the idea that this god is the only God, the Lord of all, of home and of marketplace, of sea and of land, of nation and of home. A God that has a universal claim on creation would have been a novelty to them, and it took a fairly extreme set of circumstances to get them to consider and respond to it.

Later we will think about the task that we face when we share God's name with people, but for now the focus is on realising that Christians do not have a monopoly on spirituality, on religious experience, or on belief in a god. While I was serving my curacy in Hanley, in the centre of Stoke on Trent, we did a mission survey in parts of the parish. Of the people we talked to, seven out of ten reported having had some form of spiritual experience. None of these was attending church regularly. During our second year in Priorslee, we distributed postcards to every house in the area letting people know that we were praying for them and inviting them to get in touch if there was something specific that they would like us to pray for. One lady telephoned me to say how much she appreciated receiving the card, and that she was glad of our prayers. She described herself as spiritual but not religious.

Sometimes I get the sense that Christians, including myself, feel that this is a problem. We tend to talk in derogatory terms about "pick-and-mix", "contentless", or "vacuous" spirituality. Maybe we are cynical about a reality show contestant who describes themselves as "spiritual", or about a celebrity embracing Kaballah mysticism or Buddhism. Now, I am not suggesting that all expressions of human spirituality are healthy, but I would argue that the continuing and growing exploration of these expressions does point towards a deep need in people, and that a confident and generous Christianity can have a lot to offer in response.

In much of the thinking and writing about mission, the importance of engaging with someone's beliefs is emphasised. For some this is important because it enables us to engage in conversation with people at a place that they are nearest to faith, rather than at one where they are furthest away. Identifying the distinguishing features of a belief system, so that we can understand what aspects of Christianity will be attractive to it, and which aspects will be offensive to it, makes sense. For instance, popular physicist Professor Brian Cox has a worldview that does not include the existence of God, but he has also said, "I do think there's common ground between religion and science in that you notice that the world is beautiful and that nature is absolutely fascinating."[6] Given this, a shared wonder at the beauty of the universe might be a good place to start a conversation with a fan of the floppy-haired Professor.

For other writers, being sensitive to the spirituality and beliefs of another is important because it shows respect to a conversation partner. They would argue that it is only by being open to the possibility of being converted to another's point of view that we have the right to ask others to be open in the same way. If we are to have an honest conversation, we need to be ready to learn as much about someone else's beliefs as we want to share about ours.

However, neither of these can be demonstrated from the story of the sailors in Jonah. What we are invited to do here is to recognise something even more fundamental. The existence of a God-shaped hole in

[6] http://www.dailymail.co.uk/sciencetech/article-1262449/ Brian-Cox-pop-star-turned-pin-professor-series-solar-sent-career-orbit.html#ixzz21H6MpEwZ

every heart may be a cliché, but that is what we are being shown in this passage. God has gone before us in creation, and has created human beings to know God. Christians do not have a monopoly on spirituality, religious experience, or belief in god, and this fact points to the universal claim of God on creation. Later we will consider how we can enable people to respond to this claim, but for now the focus is on the reality that God is part of peoples' lives before we arrive.

This reality is not just seen in peoples' religious beliefs but also in their moral sense. In the Jewish tradition it is suggested that the sailors were so resistant to the idea of throwing Jonah into the sea that they tried something else first.[7] The traditional Jewish story says that they lowered him into the sea as far as his knees, and the storm abated, so they pulled him back into the boat. They storm got worse again, so they dipped him back in, up to his belly. The wind dropped and they hauled him in. The waves rose again so in he went, up to his neck. You can guess what happened next. Eventually the sailors do what

---

[7] trs. Friedlander, *Pirke de Rabbi Eliezer* (Kegan Paul, Trench, Trubner and Co Ltd, 1916), p. 69.

Jonah had told them to do in the first place, and throw him in completely.

This might be speculative, but it illustrates something that is in the Biblical account: the human decency of the sailors. They do not want to save their own skins at the expense of Jonah's life. They know that life is precious, and do all that they can to preserve it. The existence of this moral sense in the world is referred to by Paul in his letter to the church in Rome. He writes about Gentiles, those who are not seen as part of the people of God, who nevertheless behave in line with God's laws: "They show that what the law requires is written on their hearts." (Romans 2:15a)

Sometimes I think about my friends and neighbours who lead basically moral lives, and are kind and welcoming, honest and caring. Who have good marriages and raise their children with love. Who work hard and play with laughter. I think about them, and I ask myself why they might need God, and my courage for witnessing to them about the good news of Jesus drains away. There are many answers to this question, but one that has occurred to me as I write is that their very goodness is actually evidence of God's work in their lives. God created and loves our friends, work colleagues and neighbours. God has written what the law requires on their hearts, so why should we be surprised when we see evidence of this? It focuses us on the reality that God is part of peoples' lives before we arrive.

To ponder:

What makes up the belief-systems and worldviews of our families, friends, neighbours, work colleagues?

What parts of the good news does their current spirituality make them most open to?

What parts of God's call on their lives are they likely to find most difficult?

Are we willing to risk being converted to another's point of view?

What evidence do we see in other people's lives of an appreciation of right and wrong?

Conversion

*So they picked Jonah up and threw him into the sea;
and the sea ceased from its raging.* (Jonah 1:15)

Earlier we explored the religious and moral
backgrounds of the sailors. However, it is clear from
the story that neither their spirituality nor their
innate moral sense was going to save them. In order
to be rescued from the storm, they had to change their
minds and their behaviour. That is, they had to be
converted.

Our vision is for there to be a new congregation in
Priorslee. This will mostly be made up of local people
who will have come to faith in Jesus and decided to
follow him.

This vision will only come into reality if people
become Christians - if they convert to Christianity. In
fact, the only way that the church anywhere grows,
whether it is starting from scratch or is building on
foundations hundreds of years old, is by people
becoming Christians - if they convert to Christianity.
Given this, it seems to me that it is important for us to
have a good understanding of conversion, so we will

look at conversion from the perspective of all the characters that we encounter in this book.

I wonder when you last converted. In 2012 about a quarter of a million people stopped smoking with the help of the NHS Stop Smoking Service. They converted from being smokers to being non-smokers. Between 2005 and 2010 at least 2 million people converted from being people who didn't vote for a Conservative Party candidate at the General Election to being people who did. Between 2005 and 2013, 1.5 million people took up a sporting activity which they did at least once a week. They were converted from couch potatoes into sportspeople.

In all of these examples we know that the person has converted because we can see a change in their behaviour, in their pattern of life - what they do or don't do. Surveys of people who smoke usually report that about 70% of them want to stop, but that desire doesn't make them non-smokers. To be converted to being a non-smoker, something has to change in what they *do*. Similarly, there are those who disagree with things that our government does but who don't engage with their MP and may not even vote. People might believe that exercise is good for them, but unless they actually do the exercise, they will not experience the benefits of it. In all these examples, conversion is incomplete, and ineffective, unless it includes action.

When we consider the story of the people of Nineveh we will look at the importance of penitence in conversion. Penitence for past misdoings, however, is not mentioned in the story of the sailors. The process of conversion that is depicted for them in this story is one of a changed understanding about God, followed by a change in actions. Changed thinking that leads to changed doing.

As we've seen, the sailors started off believing that there was someone greater than them. Jonah told them who that someone was (more of this later) and what needed to be done. Their initial response was not one of belief. Instead of believing, they started to row for land. This proved to be pointless, so instead they changed their minds, changed their actions, and were saved because of their faith.

The idea that it is our active response to what we know of God that's important, rather than what we say we believe, is found all the way though the Bible.

In the Old Testament we hear the prophets lamenting that God's people say that they believe in God, and even come to worship, but do not do what God has commanded.[8] Jesus tells a story of two builders,[9] one of whom digs deep foundations onto rock; the other doesn't dig foundations, but builds his house on the ground. When the storms rise, the house on the rock stands firm, and the house with no foundations crumbles. The first builder is the one who hears Jesus' words and puts them into action. In the book of James we read that even the forces of evil believe that there is one God.[10] What they believe is true, but their response to it is not one that saves them. Instead, they shudder.

Each of us is on a boat, a boat called "Our Life". Our boats float along on the stream of time. At times the ride is smooth and steady, floating along in the company of other boats, other lives. We may even lash a couple of boats together. Some boats seem to encounter many storms and rapids, others drift on serenely. Whether we meet many storms or none, one

[8] For example, Isaiah 1:12-17
[9] Luke 6:46-49
[10] James 2:19

thing is certain: eventually this boat will sink. At that point we will all need to be rescued from death. No amount of hard rowing on our part will ever pull us away from the rocks.

The promise of God is that we can be rescued from those rocks. That promise is available to everybody. Jesus came to earth, navigated the stream, hit the rocks, and came up waving not drowning. It is this promise of rescue that we have to offer to those who have not heard it. It is a promise that calls for a response of changed minds and of changed actions - a promise that calls for conversion. I don't find this an easy thing to write, and I find it an even more difficult thing to say to people. But this is not a responsibility that I can duck. Of course I need to have grace in the way that I talk about these things, being sensitive to the right times and places to have these conversations. In the end, however, I am called to ask people to choose whether or not they are willing change their minds about God, and to live differently. If I don't, then not only am I being unfaithful, but I am potentially robbing them of the opportunity to make that choice.

Earlier on we thought about the way in which a

conversion is associated with a change in behaviour. Smokers become non-smokers and coach potatoes become runners. Similarly, we saw that what saved the sailors, what showed their conversion to God's way of doing things, was a change in what they were doing. They stopped rowing and threw Jonah into the sea.

There are also consequences of this kind for people who decide to follow Jesus and convert to Christianity. Jesus' story of the builders makes it clear that he expects his followers to put what he teaches into practice. To love neighbours. To love God. To forgive others. To serve the poor. To heal the sick. To be faithful. To be holy. To be generous with time and money.

It seems to me that this has to inform how we reach out to people with the good news of Jesus. We have to be clear with people that Jesus does not just invite us to agree in our heads that we believe something, and that instead he challenges us to change the way that we live. These changes are unlikely to be comfortable, and may very well lead us into conflict with people who we love and who love us. Jesus promises that the Holy Spirit will help us to realise what those changes are and when we are to make them, and that he will give us strength to see it through. Converting to Christianity means changing the way that we live, and we need to be up front and clear about this with people who are exploring what it means to follow Jesus.

We can only do this with any authenticity if it is shown in our lives. As Peter writes, we should live such good lives that people see our good deeds and glorify God. I am painfully aware that I am not perfect, and that there are many aspects of my life that don't match what I say I believe, but I do believe that the Holy Spirit is working in me so that these become less and less, and that as I follow Jesus more closely I am made able to be a better witness to his life-changing love.

One of the ways that our lives change is that we become obedient to Jesus; we put what he teaches into practice. One of the last commands that Jesus gave to his disciples was that they should go and make disciples.[11] If Jesus' disciples were to make disciples like them, then it follows that their disciples should

[11] Matthew 28:19

also make disciples, and so on down the generations. Those of us who are disciples of Jesus today have been given this command: to make disciples. We are Christians because of the obedience of generation upon generation of disciples before us in following this command. Now it is our turn to put what we believe into action.

To ponder:

When did you last change your mind about something?

How did it feel?

When did you last do something differently because you had been persuaded that it was a better way?

What convinced you?

Who has been most effective in making you in a disciple?

What was so effective about their disciple-making?

Despite Jonah

*But Jonah set out to flee to Tarshish from the presence
of the Lord. He went down to Joppa and found a ship
going to Tarshish; so he paid his fare and went on
board, to go with them to Tarshish, away from the
presence of the Lord.* (Jonah 1:3)

There is a scene in one of C.S. Lewis' Narnia chronicles
in which the young girl, Lucy, asks the Lion, Aslan,
what would have happened if she had followed a
different course of action. Aslan says to her, "Nobody
is ever told that".[12] Asking "what if?" can be a
dangerous preoccupation, as it can distract us from
dealing with the reality of the situation we actually
face. Nevertheless, it is a question that occurred to me
as I read the story of the sailors' conversions. "What if
Jonah had not disobeyed God but had gone straight to
Nineveh? Would the sailors have come to know about
the Lord?" We cannot answer this question, but what
we can say is that God worked for good in a situation
that came about because of Jonah's disobedience. God
took the sow's ear of Jonah's rebellion and made it
into the silk purse of redemption.

[12] Lewis, *Prince Caspian* (Lions, 1980), p. 125.

In Priorslee we are currently in the fairly early stages of pioneer ministry. We are doing what we can to listen to the communities that we are becoming part of. We are listening to God. We are aiming to discern what God is doing, and how we might join in. We are praying, and we believe that what we are doing is line with those prayers. However, I have a problem. I like to know that something is going to work before I do it. I'm not really very good at failure, so I am keen to know that any project we embark on is perfectly aligned with God's will. To some extent this might sound commendable, but the risk is that I will allow this desire to stop me doing anything, because I am not sure that it will succeed.

The story of the sailors encourages us to take a risk. In Paul's letter to the church in Rome he writes that God works all things together for the good of those who love him,[13] and this story gives us a concrete example of how that works in practice. I am not suggesting that the most effective mission strategy is for us to deliberately disobey God. I am suggesting that, since God used a situation brought into being by

---

[13] Romans 8:28

disobedience, how much more will God be able to use situations brought about by our best endeavours. We do not have to have every base covered before we start following him.

This reflection reinforces a particular understanding of what it means to wait upon God - a concept that is at the heart of following Jesus. In scripture we are commanded to wait upon God, and we see the positive consequences that flow from faithful waiting. We are also, however, warned against laziness, and against not making the best of the opportunities afforded to us.

Two of Jesus' parables illustrate this point. In the first he tells of ten bridesmaids at a wedding.[14] Their responsibility was to welcome the bridegroom to the wedding feast with bright lights, and they had oil lamps with them, ready to do this. Unfortunately for five of the bridesmaids, the bridegroom was later than they had expected. They ran out of oil and their lamps went out. They went to buy more, but while they were away the bridegroom arrived, and when they returned they were shut out of the feast. They had not

[14] Matthew 25:1-13

been prepared for the wait.

In another, Jesus tells of a man who is preparing to go on a journey.[15] He calls three of his servants to him. To the first he gives ten gold coins, to the second he gives five gold coins, and to the third he gives one gold coin. On his return, he calls the three servants to report back to him. The first and second have both invested wisely and doubled the money. They are praised and rewarded. The actions of the third are not so well appreciated. He has hidden the money and waited for his master's return. The man is displeased at this servant's fear and lack of action and dismisses him. The servant should not have waited.

In some ways, this is about the relationship that we explored earlier between faithful prayer and believing action. We are called to wait, but the waiting we are called to is not passive but active and, most importantly, attentive. It is the waiting of a table attendant who is still, focussed on observing the one being served, ready to pour the wine, bring a fresh napkin, clear an empty plate. It is the attentiveness of the lover who is a student of the beloved, knowing

[15] Matthew 25:14-30

how she likes her tea in the morning, when she needs to talk something through, when he needs to be given some space.[16]

So, we are to be attentive to God. This will find expression and be deepened in spiritual disciplines, in prayer, worship, and Bible reading, both on our own and with others. As we wait attentively on God, we will learn to move with the Spirit and in the direction of God's heart. Sometimes we might be caught napping, or be a little over-eager, but as we return our focus to God, so we will be able to get back in step. As we get better at this we will grow in confidence to embark on things in faith, not having to have every base covered in advance.

Not only do we not have to have every base covered, but we can actually afford to fail. We are human, and not yet made perfect, and will still sin. It is likely that we will fall out with people, mishandle situations, and generally screw up. If we are not careful, the fear of the possibility of these failures, or the shame we feel about them when we have done them, will do more

[16] Fincher & Fincher, *Coffee Shop Conversations* (Zondervan, 2010), p. 107.

damage to our mission than the sins themselves. We should, absolutely, aim to live lives of such holiness that people are drawn to God. But when we fail we need to remember that the good news that we are bringing is news of forgiveness, and we need to live in the reality of that good news ourselves. Now, there are moral failings that do disqualify people from public ministry for a season, or even permanently. This is not because God has not forgiven them, but because there is soul work for them to do that cannot be done safely whilst leading others.

However, there are many situations in which we may fail or sin in a way which does not mean that we need to step out of ministry, but which we do need to know that God has forgiven us for, remembering that God can work every situation for good. The story of the way God worked in the lives of the sailors, despite Jonah's disobedience, can be an encouragement to us in these times.

This section has been a bit tangential to the story of Jonah and the sailors who accompanied him. A reflection on that story has been a springboard for us to consider something that is not derived from it. So let us return to the sea for a final illustration. A ship cannot be steered if it is moving at the same speed as the water it is on. For a rudder to work, for it to able to change the direction of travel of the boat, it has to have water flowing past it. If the boat is travelling at the same speed as the water, then there is no flow over the rudder, the water around it moves along with it, and there is no steering. For us to be given direction by God, then it is necessary for us to be moving at a different speed to the water around us. Sometimes that will mean that we need to be still, holding station against the thrust of the prevailing stream. At other times it will mean moving more quickly, our sails full of the wind of the Spirit.

To ponder:

Can you see times in your own life where God has worked difficult situations for good?

What do you find most difficult about waiting?

What do you find difficult about risking action?

Are you more tempted to premature action or to needless indecision?

What talents is God calling you to invest wisely today?

Chapter 2

The Fish

Sanctuary

But the Lord provided a great fish to swallow up Jonah...
(Jonah 1:17a)

How bad does your situation have to be for the belly of a fish to be an improvement? All Jonah had done since he left home was to get deeper and deeper into trouble. He went down to Joppa, got down into the boat, went down into the lowest parts of the ship, fell into a deep sleep, and finally was thrown down into the ocean where the deep closed around him. He was about as low as you can get, and at the very bottom of his fall the Lord gave him a respite, a safe place, a sanctuary.

In modern English the word sanctuary has come to mean any place of safety, shelter, and healing. We have animal sanctuaries for mistreated donkeys. We have health spas and rehabilitation centres called "Sanctuary". Many people have places they think of as their sanctuary, somewhere they can get a bit of peace and quiet from the hustle and bustle of life. Maybe a garden shed, a favourite cafe, the daily cup of tea in the kitchen between dropping the kids off at school and starting on the day's work, a stop at McDonald's between one customer meeting and another. A sanctuary.

The idea of a sanctuary being a place of safety comes from the ancient tradition that someone who was being chased, either by a lynch mob or an officer of the law, might go into a place of worship - a sanctuary - and be safe. The safety that this gave them came from three sources. Firstly, they were appealing to the god of the place to judge between them and their pursuers. Their willingness to run the risk of being found guilty in an eternal court demonstrated their strength of conviction that they were innocent. Secondly, they were placing themselves under the protection of the god of the place, showing their faith in that god's power to be a secure refuge for them. Thirdly, they were appealing to the belief of their pursuers that a place of worship is a sacred place, not to be polluted by human blood spilt in anger. The important point to appreciate here is that the word sanctuary originally indicated a place in which a god was thought to be present, and which, because of this primary meaning, came to mean a place of safety.

This is illustrated by a consideration of the place of worship for the people of God. In the book of Exodus, after the people of God have been rescued from Egypt, they are given instructions about how to set up a place to worship God, where God will be present. It is in the midst of these instructions that we hear God say to Moses, "And have them make me a sanctuary, so that I may dwell among them." (Exodus 25:8) This sanctuary is to be a special place where God is present, and which is made so holy by this presence that only certain priests can enter it at certain times. This sanctuary was portable: it was in a tent and moved around with the people of God as they journeyed to and across the promised land. Eventually the sanctuary, the Ark of the Covenant, and its attendant

altar, all settled in Jerusalem, during the reign of King
David. When David's life was drawing towards its end,
there was an attempted coup to prevent his son
Solomon inheriting the throne. The coup was
unsuccessful and we read that the ring leader,
Adonijah, headed for the place of worship, the
sanctuary, and grabbed onto the altar, claiming
immunity from any revenge that Solomon might have
been planning.[17] So we see that the sanctuary is firstly
the place of the presence of God, and that only
because it is a place of worship is it a place of safety,
healing, and peace.

It is from this place that Jonah was fleeing. "But Jonah
set out to flee to Tarshish from the presence of the
LORD." (Jonah 1:3) He was trying to get away from
God and the worship of God, and away from the
commission of God on his life. In doing so he left the
place of safety, his refuge from the storms, the place of
his security. He left himself vulnerable - and, as we
have discovered, he found himself at the bottom of a
hole, out of his depth, and drowning. But he didn't end
up there. God gave him a new sanctuary, right where

[17] 1 Kings 1:50-51

he was. The belly of the fish was a place of safety for Jonah because he recognised it as a sanctuary in the truest sense, a place of God's presence, and he responded to this presence in worship.

This story is one of the hints in the Old Testament that God's presence might be more widely encountered than in specially set-aside places. This idea is vividly expressed in the words of the psalmist: "Where can I go from your spirit? Or where can I flee from your presence?" (Psalm 139:7) Nevertheless, the persistent belief that God's presence is linked strongly with a specific place of worship is demonstrated by the desire of the exiled people of God to return to Jerusalem in order to rebuild the temple and reinstate temple worship. It was this rebuilt temple that was the temple Jesus knew during his life on earth. In his life, he brought the presence of God outside the temple, beyond the set-aside place of worship. At the time of his death the curtain which veiled the holiest part of the sanctuary ripped in two, from top to bottom.[18] It is as though God reached down from heaven and destroyed the physical barrier that

[18] Matthew 27:51

symbolised the spiritual barrier between humanity and God.

In one sense this means that the wider application of the word sanctuary is completely fitting. If the belly of a fish can be a true sanctuary, then so can a garden shed, a kitchen table, or a McDonald's. In another sense I feel that we are missing something if we fail to realise that it is the presence of God that makes a sanctuary truly safe, and if we fail to realise that knowing the presence of God will lead us to worship. When we meet people who are going through storms in life, and who may be drowning, we have good news for them: that there is a place of safety, of peace, and of refuge. There is a sanctuary. It isn't a special set-aside place - it can be experienced anywhere. But there is only one way in.

The reason that Adonijah grabbed hold of the altar to claim protection from Solomon was because it was the place of sacrifice. It was the place that blood was spilt. The temple altar with its repeated sacrifices has now been done away with by the ultimate sacrifice. Blood no longer needs to be spilt on the altar because Jesus' blood was spilt on the cross. By giving up his life he enabled people to be adopted into God's family and to come into their Father's presence, and to be safe and secure there. Jesus opened this gate for people, but we have to choose to walk through it. We have to grab hold of the place of sacrifice, the place where blood was spilt - the cross of Jesus - and claim its power and protection over our lives. In this sanctuary we are declared innocent in the eternal courts by the Judge of all, we are placed under the protection of the Mighty Lord of the Armies of Heaven, we are made holy, and we are drawn into worship.

The good news that there is a true sanctuary, in which anybody can be safe and secure, has another, less comfortable, implication.

There are places where people feel safe which are not actually secure. One of the most difficult things to do is to persuade someone to leave a place in which they *feel* safe so they can reach a place where they will actually *be* safe. This is especially so when the person has to do something risky to get from the place of perceived safety to the place of actual safety. It is daunting, but it is part of our mission to call people from places where they feel safe into a place of true sanctuary, where they will be safe for ever.

To ponder:

Do you have a place of sanctuary?

Are you aware of God's presence there?

What is the most unexpected place in which you have experienced a sense of sanctuary?

What storms do you observe in the lives of your friends and neighbours?

What false sanctuaries do you have?

What false sanctuaries do you see in your neighbourhood?

What do people have to risk if they are to leave those false sanctuaries?

How might you invite them to enter the sanctuary that God has provided for them?

Now and Not Yet

...and Jonah was in the belly of the fish for three days and three nights. (Jonah 1:17b)

Asking people to leave the places that *feel* safe so they can move to a place that actually *is* safe is challenging, because the place we are suggesting they move to doesn't always *look* very safe. The security of the sanctuary has to be taken on trust, and moving to it demands an act of faith. I believe it to be a reasonable act of faith, but it is an act of faith nevertheless.

The story is told of a man climbing in the mountains. Ascending through the clouds on a steep and icy path, he slips. As he is tumbling down the cliff, his flailing hand grabs a small tree rooted in a crevice in the rock. He catches his breath and starts calling for help. At first no one answers, but at last there is a voice drifting down through the mist towards him. "Let go". The voice goes on to explain that he is a mountain guide for the area and knows that there is a ledge a couple of metres below the place where the mountaineer is hanging. If he lets go he will land safely on it and be able to await rescue. The man looks down, and all he can see is swirling mist. He has to make a decision. It would be reasonable to let go, but it would still be an act of faith.

One of the reasons that this jump is difficult is because the sanctuary available to us now is, in some senses, temporary. The belly of the fish was not Jonah's final place of safety; it was the place in which he was transported to the beach, dry land, and actual safety. There is a sense in which our Christian lives on this earth are like this. We have been saved from the storm, but we have not yet been delivered to the beach. We believe that our eventual safety is secure, but we have to be honest and say that at the moment the belly of the fish may very well be dark and stink horribly.

In the belly of the fish we live out the "now and not yet" of our walk with Jesus. We are now safe in God's arms and are not yet safe from the hurts of this world. We are now princes and princesses of the Kingdom of Heaven and are not yet wearing our crowns. We are now being made whole in Christ and are not yet completely whole. There is now healing of some disease and illness, and not yet healing of all infirmity. Jesus is now victorious over death and has not yet had his victory march. We are now holy in God's sight and are not yet holy in our day-to-day living.

A powerful expression of this sense of "now and not yet" is found in this reflection by Philip Yancey:

"Good Friday and Easter Sunday have earned names on the calendar. Yet in a real sense we live on Saturday, the day with no name. What the disciples experienced on a small scale – three days of grief over one man who had died on a cross – we now live through on a cosmic scale. Human history grinds on between the time of promise and fulfilment. Can we trust that God can make something holy and beautiful and good out of a world that includes Bosnia and Rwanda and inner-city ghettos and jammed prisons in the richest nation on earth? It's Saturday on planet Earth. Will Sunday ever come?"[19]

This idea, if we are willing to consider it honestly, can provide a rich resource for us to engage with some of the questions that people have about the Christian faith. For instance, somebody might object to the truth claims of Jesus because they know that some of their

[19] Yancey, *The Jesus I Never Knew* (Zondervan, 1995). Use by permission of Zondervan. www.zondervan.com

Christian friends get drunk with them every Friday night. In this case we might be tempted to disown our brothers and sisters: "they're probably not real Christians." If we do this, then we had better be pretty certain that there is nothing in our lives which might lead Jesus to disown us on the last day. A more fruitful path might be to talk about the "now and not yet" of Christian life, explaining that none of us are the finished article and that we all have imperfections, but that all followers of Jesus are committed to becoming more like him and following his ways more closely. Everybody is welcome to join us on this journey, knowing that as we stumble and fall we can help each other up.

This is not licence for us to continue sinning. We do all have a responsibility to be the best witnesses we can be for Jesus, to be the most attractive ambassadors. However, we will fail. "Now and not yet" gives us a language to talk about those failures that neither minimises their seriousness nor sets us up on a "holier than thou" pedestal. It allows us to walk alongside others in authenticity, sharing the struggles of our lives, and offering to others the strength that God gives us in those struggles.

This idea can also give us a way of enabling people to lament, to complain about, and to mourn for the things that grieve them. It seems to me that we sometimes don't know what to do with Holy Saturday. The agape meal of Maundy Thursday has been shared, the curtain has gone down on the drama and processions of Good Friday, and the dawn service, bacon butties, and celebration of Easter Sunday are yet to come. We might organise picnics or Easter egg hunts, or just go shopping. Perhaps we decide that we need to organise outreach activities for that day because everybody goes to their families on Easter Sunday.

While I was in Stoke, we decided to spend a couple of hours on Holy Saturday walking around the desolate areas of the city on a pilgrimage of lament. We toured the terraces that had been ripped out as the first stage of a stalled regeneration plan. We visited the run-down shopping precinct by the crumbing bus station. We looked over odd-shaped pieces of land in the middle of housing estates that are inconvenient to redevelop. We stopped at the site of a proposed termination suite. At different places we prayed, anointed land with oil, and built a cairn. It seemed a fitting way to spend the day which is such a strong expression of "now and not yet".

I wonder if we might all do things a bit differently and make Holy Saturday a gift to our communities as a space to lament. This is something unique that Jesus' people have to offer to the world. Chocolates and spring flowers are coming out of peoples' ears. Easter egg hunts are organised by schools, garden centres, and wildlife sanctuaries. Craft activities are available down at the library and the soft play centre. I can think of few others who will say, "We know what it's like to be in a place where it's dark and it stinks. We have hope, but we will be real with you and give you space to complain about it." There is a place for doing all the other things, but let us not lose sight of one of the distinctive things that we can say at Easter. This is a time to acknowledge that we live in a world which is broken. That we are waiting. We are in the belly of a fish. There is no dressing it up. We have a certain hope for the future but at the moment it's dark and it stinks.

To ponder:

How might you use the idea of "now and not yet" to engage with someone who asks why, if there is a God, there is so much pain in the world?

What do you do on Holy Saturday?

When did you last lament on behalf of your community?

What is dark and stinking about your life?

What of the "now" have you experienced that has increased your hope and faith that you will see the "not yet"?

Resurrection

The waters closed in over me; the deep surrounded me; weeds were wrapped around my head at the roots of the mountains. I went down to the land whose bars closed upon me forever; yet you brought up my life from the Pit, O Lord my God. (Jonah 2:5-6)

The appearance of the fish in the story of Jonah is the part that most assaults our sense of reality, unless our senses are so dulled by repetition of the story that we are no longer shocked. Up until this point, we might have been nodding along with what seems to be a fairly ho-hum morality tale about the consequences of not doing what God tells us to do. Then the surreal breaks in. A fish appears and swallows the main character. A fish! This makes for great Sunday School material, but it might also stop us engaging with the narrative fully because it seems to move it into the realm of the Just So story.[20]

Up until now we have not thought in any detail about the historicity of the story of Jonah. This is because

[20] Especially that of the Whale and the ship-wrecked Mariner – he of the infinite-resource-and-sagacity.

the insights that it can give us into mission are independent of whether or not the events described actually happened. Furthermore, a detailed discussion of the various views on this would be a distraction from that main focus. However, it seems to me that while there are good grounds for thinking that Jonah was written some centuries after the events described, there is little reason to think that the events it describes have no basis in historical fact.

I mention this here because it is at this point, at the appearance of the fish, that the temptation is strongest to doubt the historicity of the narrative.

It is so flagrant it is embarrassing. It flies in the face of all we know about how the world works. Despite this, there have been valiant attempts to identify a fish or whale that could physically swallow a man and disgorge him whole three days later. These are fairly pointless. They attempt to rationalise and explain the miraculous. The whole point of the miraculous is that it is only explicable by the sovereign action of God.

Neither can the fish be swept under the carpet. It is not a little amusing interlude in the middle of the story, a filler between the main action on the ship and in Nineveh. It is in the middle of story, making the central point of the story explicitly, and it is not coincidental that it is the most difficult part of the story to believe. The central point, the main point of the story, is one of resurrection; of God's power to bring life from death. The sailors and the people of Nineveh experience this power, and Jonah praises God for it as he experiences it in the belly of the fish.

Some months after I was ordained as a priest I had to ask myself seriously whether I believed in the resurrection. Week after week, as I broke the bread and poured the wine at the Lord's Table, I would proclaim the resurrection. As I did this I was struck again and again by how foolish this seems to the world. I have never known anybody who rose from the dead. I don't think that I know anybody who knows somebody who has been raised from the dead. The resurrection of Jesus from the dead is, if we stop to think about it, completely shocking. It is an event entirely outside the observed and lived experience of the vast majority of the billions of people who have ever lived. People who die stay dead. They do not return to life. To suggest otherwise is to make a claim that is an unutterably cruel false hope unless it is true.

There is good evidence for the death and resurrection of Jesus. There is the reliable documentary evidence from eyewitnesses of the risen Christ. There is the observable difference that the resurrection appearances made in the lives of the followers of Jesus. There is the observable difference that the risen life of Jesus has made in the lives of people through the ages. All of this is good evidence, which makes the belief that Jesus rose from the dead a reasonable faith. However, it is good to be reminded that it does require faith, and that there are also strong reasons for those who do not share that faith to think that it is foolish.

Resurrection is important to mission for a couple of reasons. The first, and primary, one is that it provides justification for a message of hope. Jesus was raised from the dead, defeating death for all who follow in his way. Whatever has gone before in a life, whatever darkness, sin, trauma, or abuse we have known is dead in Jesus, and there can be new life for all. Earlier on I suggested that we need to recapture the unique gift of Holy Saturday, an opportunity to be real about the "now and not yet" of life on earth. Even more than this, we must be bold about the message of Easter

Sunday. Christ is risen. He is risen indeed. Praise God.

There is a second reason that resurrection is important to mission, and it is a little more subtle. Resurrection is not only the climax of the Christian story but also a controlling theme of Christian faith, action, and mission. Jesus' death and resurrection not only opened up the way to life for us, but also provide a pattern for the way we are to live. This reality has to shape both the content and the form of our mission. We know that content and form in communication are inextricably linked - that the medium is the message[21] - but sometimes it is helpful to think about them separately before using the insights we have gained to understand how they combine.

In terms of the content of what we say to people, the resurrection is good news. Because of Jesus' resurrection, there is hope of life in all its fullness, now and forever in God's family. Death does not have to be the end, because Jesus has defeated death. We have already seen that these claims are big claims which can be difficult to believe, but they are claims of

[21] A phrase coined by Marshall McLuhan, *Understanding Media: the extensions of man* (McGraw-Hill, 1964).

hope, which we can make with confidence. We also need to bear in mind, however, that there are costly implications to the good news of the resurrection. There is a prerequisite to being raised from the dead and that is: being dead. We know that we will all physically die, and that because of Jesus' defeat of death it is possible for us to be raised to life from our physical death. However, there is more to it than this.

As Jesus was heading towards Jerusalem in the last days of his life on earth, he shared with his friends some of what was coming.[22] In the biblical account, he starts off by talking about the way in which a seed has to be planted if there is to be a harvest. If a farmer wants grain to sell next year, there is no point in him putting all his seed-corn into a bag and keeping it in the shed. He has to plant it. The seed has to die in the ground so that new, fruitful life can come from it. At this point it would be possible to think that Jesus is just talking about himself, since he only mentions a single grain of wheat falling to the ground. What he says next, however, opens it up to include us. He says that "anyone who loves their life will lose it, while

[22] John 12:23-26

anyone who hates their life in this world will keep it
for eternal life. Whoever serves me must follow me;
and where I am, my servant also will be." With those
"anyones" and the "whoever," Jesus is talking to us
and to those with whom we are sharing his message.

As we invite people to consider walking with us in
Jesus' way, we should be confident and bold about the
hope and joy that is to be found in the resurrection.
We should also be honest about the fact that this way
is a costly one to walk. Jesus went to the cross, and we
are called to follow him. Jesus laid down his life, and
we are called to follow him. The road to resurrection
always goes by way of the cross.

In terms of the form of how we communicate with
people, and carry out our mission, this understanding
of resurrection is critical. In order to open up the way
for others to be able to hear what Jesus is saying to
them, and able to develop ways of engaging with the
reality of God in their lives through worship, we will
have to be willing to die to ourselves and our own
preferences.[23] This means that we plant churches and
launch ministries which meet the needs of the people

[23] See *Mission-Shaped Church* (Church House Publishing, 2004).

to whom we are sent, rather than moving out of churches that we find a bit dull in order to spice up our own lives. It means that we may have to allow some of our precious historical buildings, practices, and privileges to die in order for new growth to come.

Jesus was the perfect integration of form and content in communication. He laid down his heavenly life to come to earth as a man, and he laid down his earthly life on the cross. He was raised to life on earth and then ascended to heaven. He showed us the way he taught us to live. If we are to be authentic in our invitation to others to this life, we must issue that invitation not just with our lips but with our whole lives, laid down. It is then that we will see new life and fruitfulness; true resurrection.

To ponder:

Do you believe in resurrection?

What objections to the historical fact of Jesus' resurrection have you come across?

What things have you been willing to see die because you had faith that doing so created the possibility of new growth?

What in your Christian tradition would you find most difficult to lay down or to see die?

How do you celebrate Easter Sunday?

Conversion

Then the Lord spoke to the fish, and it spewed Jonah out upon the dry land. (Jonah 2:10)

Perhaps it might sound a bit odd to consider the fish as having experienced conversion, but there is no disputing the fact that at one point in its life it decided that swallowing Jonah would be good, and at another point that it decided to reverse that decision and vomit Jonah out. This might be pushing it; after all, it is clear that the whole process was under God's direction. Nevertheless, we will discuss God's conversion later, and so it is possible that the agent of God's action can also be described as undergoing a change of mind, experiencing conversion. Furthermore, this idea gives us the opportunity to reflect on vomiting and conversion.

We vomit because there is something in the stomach that the body doesn't want there. This might be poison, bad food, or a bacterial infection. It might just be that our body can't cope with the work of digestion and needs to shut down the system. Vomiting is generally involuntary, but we can stimulate it if we need to - for instance, if we believe that we've swallowed something dangerous. Although it is unpleasant, our ability to vomit is a really important one, and can save our lives. Because of the strength of their stomach valve and angle of their food pipe, horses are unable to vomit. Because of this, colic – stomach problems – can be fatal for them. If, despite its unpleasantness, physical vomiting is good for us - even life-saving - then it seems reasonable to suggest that spiritual vomiting might also be critical to our spiritual health.[24]

The first way in which spiritual vomiting is good for us is when we purge out sin. When we come to faith we come with a lifetime of sin which, if it is not dealt with, can continue to cause havoc in our lives. There are churches which believe that one of the most significant steps a new Christian can take is to make a fearless moral inventory and confess those sins explicitly to another person. The rationale of these communities, based on experience, is that this process allows a person to be honest about who they are and

[24] I am aware that physical vomiting is not always good for us. Bulimia is a life-threatening condition that should never be taken lightly. I discuss the spiritual parallels of this later.

the baggage that they come with.[25] It also gives a strong ethos within those church communities of mutual accountability and togetherness in the ongoing battle with sin in our lives. It is acknowledged that it is likely, as Christians mature, that they will become more aware of their previous sinfulness, and therefore realise that they have further things to repent of. It is felt that this is more likely to happen if the habit of self-examination and confession is introduced early in a Christian's life. The longer it is left, in fact, the less likely it is to develop at all.

The second way that spiritual vomiting is good for us is in the getting rid of bad habits, resisting temptation, and combating sins that beset us. This is the ongoing work of sanctification: becoming more like Jesus under the guidance and shaping of the Holy Spirit. If we have a bad habit, something that we do repetitively which damages either ourselves or others, then it has to be broken. Part of breaking that habit is vomiting out - getting rid of - the things that are entwined with it. If it is an addiction such as pornography, smoking, or alcohol then this may

---

[25] For example, Reeves, *Refuge* (Kregel, 2010).

involve throwing out the physical things associated with it. The books, the magazines, the cigarettes, the bottles. If it is a habit of heart or mind then there may be wrong attitudes to be confessed and relinquished.

Adrian Plass[26] tells the story of a woman who realised that her nodding acquaintance with a man who caught the same train to work as her had progressed into a friendship and was now starting to develop into a tender affection. She did not want to succumb to the temptation to be unfaithful to her husband by allowing the relationship to develop further. She started catching a later train. She vomited away the circumstances that provided the opportunity for temptation. Or, as Jesus put it, "she plucked out her eye" (Mark 9:47).

The third way in which spiritual vomiting, particularly associated with conversion, is good for us is in our getting rid of stuff. At one stage in his travels, Paul stayed for a few years in the city of Ephesus, teaching and preaching about Jesus.[27] Whilst he was there a group of people who had various occult practices

[26] Plass, *View from a Bouncy Castle* (Fount,1991), p. 16ff.
[27] Acts 19:1-20

came to believe in Jesus. One of the first things that they did was to burn all their books and equipment - the original bonfire of the vanities. Earlier we thought about the necessity of throwing away things associated with addictions and bad habits, but this is wider than that. It might be informed by the fearless moral inventory discussed above. It is about destroying the physical things that might provide a foothold for our enemy in our lives.

For different people this will include different things. In his letter to the church in Rome, Paul makes it clear that people find different things a barrier to living faithfully in Jesus' way. Writing this has reminded me that there are books in my house that I need to get rid of. For some people, they would probably not be harmful to read, but I know that their combination of sex and violence is not good for my thought-life. The trouble is, if I keep them in the house, a few months down the road, when I'm hunting round for something to read I might decide that they weren't that bad and start reading again, be drawn in by the plot, and before I know it my imagination is being polluted again.

This process isn't one that is only for individuals. The

community has a part to play as well. In an atmosphere of trust we can help each other to identify what might need to go. We might also, as a community, decide to get rid of something from our shared life together, in order to support those who find that thing a temptation. I used to take communion into a warden-supported accommodation for the elderly. One week one of the ladies took me aside and told me that another of the residents wanted to receive communion but couldn't because she was a recovering alcoholic. We had a conversation about the various possibilities, and the group decided that they would rather have an alcohol-free alternative to wine so that they could all take part in the meal in unity. This is another example of what it means to die to self.

Vomiting is normally good for us. Sometimes it is not. Sometimes it becomes part of an uncontrollable, life-destroying condition. This condition often has at its root a massively distorted self-image, rock bottom self-esteem, or mental health issues. This can be as true for spiritual vomiting as for physical vomiting. Once we have vomited once, confessed our sin, and cleared our lives we are forgiven. In seeking to enable people to be free of past sin by encouraging them to engage with the reality of it, we must be careful that we do not allow them to be bound by the memory of it. When people come to faith they are adopted as children into the family of God. They are princes and princesses of God's kingdom. That is the reality of their identity. Living in that reality requires them to confess their sin and vomit away some things. It also means that they are forgiven, are free from that sin, and can walk free with their head held high.

To ponder:

If you feel sick, do you welcome the relief of vomiting or try and put it off as long as possible?

How do you feel about the thought of confessing your sins to another person?

Have you ever been aware of a habit or pattern of life, maybe not bad in itself, which had the potential to lead you into temptation?

Can you think of a time when it was important, or would have been a good idea, to get rid of something?

What would you find it difficult to give up, in your worshipping life together with others, in order to make it easier for someone else to join in more fully?

Chapter 3

The Inhabitants of Nineveh

Enemies

But this was very displeasing to Jonah, and he became angry. (Jonah 4:1)

One of the questions that came up most often as different groups reflected on this story was, "Why was Jonah so angry?"

There are always two aspects to why someone is angry. Firstly there is the situation, whatever is going on that is creating the opportunity for anger. Secondly, there is the mindset of the person, the way that they understand what is going on and how it affects them. We will look in a later section at what might have been going on in Jonah's heart when he gets angry; at this point, though, we are going to think about Jonah's situation, and in particular the fact that the people of Nineveh were the enemy.

The first mention of Nineveh in the Bible is in a list of the descendants of Noah.[28] According to this account, Nineveh was founded by Nimrod, a mighty warrior, a descendent of Noah's son Ham. However, the people of Israel were descended from Abraham, a descendent of one of Noah's other sons, Shem. This might seem insignificant to us, but this family tree reveals something that would have been deeply embedded in Jonah's mind. The people of Nineveh were warriors by blood, and whilst they received the covenant promise God made to Noah not to destroy the world again by flooding, they were outside the covenant promise of God to Abraham. They were not part of God's chosen people: they were not "one of us".

Many centuries pass before Assyria, the country of Nineveh, reappears in the history of the people of God. Abraham receives the covenant promise that his children will be God's people, a blessing to the world.

[28] Genesis 10

Abraham's great-grandson, Joseph, with his dream coat, paves the way for the people to move to Egypt. Over the years they prosper so fruitfully that the Egyptians get anxious, beginning to oppress and enslave them. God sends Moses to rescue them. They cross the Red Sea on dry land and are led through the desert to the Promised Land. Eventually they follow Joshua into the land to claim their inheritance. They live as independent tribes, led by Judges like Gideon, Deborah, and Samson. In time they decide that they need a king, and Saul, the first king of God's people, is chosen and crowned. He is followed by the great kings: David and Solomon. After Solomon's death the nation splits in two. The northern kingdom, Israel, with its capital in Samaria; and the southern kingdom, Judah, with its capital in Jerusalem.

Just over two hundred years later, around 745 BC, it is recorded[29] that King Menahem of Israel paid King Pul of Assyria a thousand talents of silver not to invade his country. This bribe, however, seems only to have whetted the Assyrians' appetite, and more and more tribute was extorted until they finally overran Israel

[29] 2 Kings 15:19

in 722 BC and forced the people into exile. This is not the only evidence that exists of the kind of relationship that existed between Israel and Assyria at this time. The first tribute paid by a king of Israel to a king of Assyria is recorded on the Black Obelisk of Shalmaneser, which shows that in 841BC King Jehu paid tribute to King Shalmaneser III.[30]

We know that the story of Jonah is set around this time because he is mentioned as a prophet who was active in Israel in the chapter preceding Menahem's payment in 2 Kings.[31] Jonah lived in a time when Assyria was relentlessly expanding, invading other countries and demanding payment from those nations over which it held sway. Nineveh was a major city of this aggressive neighbour which caused so much pain and hardship for Jonah's people. The people of Nineveh were Jonah's enemies.

Jesus said something about enemies once. He told his followers to love their enemies and to pray for those

[30]http://www.britishmuseum.org/explore/highlights/highlight_o bjects/me/t/black_obelisk_of_shalmaneser.aspx
[31] 2 Kings 14:25

who persecute them.[32] In order for us to be able to obey this command, it is important for us to be honest about who our enemies are.

There are different ways in which we might experience enmity for people. There are faceless enemies who are at a distance and who seem to have a lot of power, and over whom we seem to have little influence. These enemies include governments whose policies are unjust, corporations whose advertising is dehumanising, and media organisations whose agenda is unholy. There are also personal enemies who have caused pain to family or friends, who oppose what we are aiming to achieve, or who have failed to fulfil their obligations of care. In addition there are those who we just don't like; those we can't get on with or find personally difficult. Denying that these people are our enemies means that we start the mission to them - which God has called us to carry out - from a dishonest place. Acknowledging the enmity, and understanding it, enables us as we try to better communicate of the good news of Jesus.

This begins, as does all mission, in prayer. We pray for

[32] Matthew 5:44

our enemies, and we love them. This does not mean submitting to them, doormat-like, it means working for their good. We may feel that we cannot change the policies of faceless organisations or governments. Reconciliation in South Africa and Northern Ireland, the success of the Jubilee 2000 campaign against majority-world debt, and the growing availability of Fairtrade products are all examples of situations in which mighty enemies were and are being brought closer to the Kingdom of God by the small steps of many people in prayer and in action.

We are also called to model good ways of relating to those with whom we are in conflict. This can feel really counterintuitive, particularly when we are in the early stages of getting to know people, and be known, in a community. What do we do when life's circumstances bring us into conflict with another community stakeholder, such as a property developer, a school, or a police representative? One way would be to back away from the conflict, sacrificing our interests so that we avoid being seen as troublemakers in the community, and do not risk relationships with people that we might want to be able to work with at a later date. Perhaps this is too passive, and actually counterproductive for the health of the community in the long run. Perhaps it is better for us to stiffen our sinews, take a brave pill, and be assertive in the conviction that it is better for people to deal honestly (and gently) with each other than to allow bitterness to fester.

In addition to our human enemies there is another enemy for us to bear in mind; a spiritual enemy. In one of his letters to some of the first Christians, Jesus' friend Peter writes about an enemy that prowls around like a lion, looking for people to devour.[33] This enemy is the devil, the one who has opposed God's purpose for creation since the beginning of time. Satan, the one who lies, tempts, and accuses. The evil one, who sows discord and hates peace.[34]

When thinking about mission, there are two facets of the devil's enmity that we need to be aware of. The first is that Satan is the enemy of those to whom we have been sent. Jesus describes him as the one who

[33] 1 Peter 5:8

[34] That "the devil", "Satan", and "the evil one" are all Biblical names for the same being is shown by their usage in the otherwise parallel accounts of the explanation of the parable of the sower in Matthew 13:19, Mark 4:15, and Luke 8:12.

comes and snatches away the seeds of the good news that have been sown in peoples' hearts.[35] He initiated the rebellion of humankind against God, he opposed Jesus' mission to make reconciliation possible, and he will do all that he can to disrupt the realisation of that reconciliation. When we choose to reach out to people and share with them the freedom that is theirs in Christ, we are putting ourselves in the firing line of the one who is holding them captive. This is not to scare us off, but to take seriously the fact that mission is costly, and should not be undertaken lightly.

The second facet of the devil's enmity is his hatred of us personally. This is present, whether or not we are active in mission. Not only are we God's creation, and therefore subject to the hatred of Satan, but we have been freed from his captivity and have a privileged place as heirs to the Kingdom of God, a Kingdom from which he was expelled. As such, it should come as no surprise when we experience the onslaughts of his displeasure: temptations, lies, accusations, doubts, self-hatred, fear. Again, these warnings are not to cause us to fear, but to recognise the costly nature of

[35] Mark 4:15

following Jesus, both for ourselves and for those that we are inviting to walk in this way.

The good news is that we have not been left defenceless. Jesus gave authority to his followers to overcome all the power of the enemy.[36] Paul, in his letter to the church at Ephesus, gives us the image of a soldier putting on his kit for battle.[37]

The belt of truth, holding everything together with integrity and strength. The breastplate of righteousness that protects the heart. The sandals of readiness to share the good news with others, rescuing people from the enemy's clutches and winning more warriors for Christ. The shield of faith, joined with others in shield-walls to defend each other and to attack the enemy. The helmet of salvation, which identifies Jesus' soldiers and protects our thinking. The sword of the spirit, the word of God, the Bible, which contains all that we need to become part of the family of God. We have been given the equipment we need for the mission we have been given. It is up to us to use it faithfully on behalf of our

[36] Luke 10:19
[37] Ephesians 6:13-17

human enemies against our shared spiritual enemy.

To ponder:

Who are your enemies?

What steps could you take to bring your faceless enemies closer to the Kingdom of God?

Who are you in personal conflict with at the moment?

How do you feel that you are handling it?

What are implications of this conflict for Jesus' reputation?

How do you keep alert against the schemes of the evil one?

Which part of your soldier's kit do you feel least competent with?

What will you do to exercise with it?

Follow my Leader

And the people of Nineveh believed God; they proclaimed a fast, and everyone, great and small, put on sackcloth. When the news reached the king of Nineveh, he rose from his throne, removed his robe, covered himself in sackcloth, and sat in ashes.
(Jonah 3:5-6)

Sometimes I misread the Bible. I come to it with blinkers in place and the blinkers mean that I fail to notice things. In fact, it's worse than that. Sometimes the things that I miss are the things that would shake the blinkers away, and my vision is so distorted that I believe, wrongly, that what I've read actually reinforces my position. This happened to me the first few times that I read these verses with the home groups. I believed it said that the King led the people in repentance. It took someone in one of those groups to point out to me that actually it was the people who led the King in repentance. Getting this right is quite important in understanding how communities come to faith.

So, what were the blinkers that prevented me reading these verses correctly? What preconceptions about how communities come to faith was I carrying that were distorting my thinking? I was wrongly applying a very useful, Biblical, concept: "people of peace".

On a couple of different occasions during his time on earth, we see Jesus decide that it is time for the disciples to have a bit of a field trip.[38] Each expedition is an opportunity for them to go and get some practical experience of putting into practice the things that he's been showing them and teaching them. He sends them out, in pairs, to the surrounding towns and villages to heal the sick and to tell people about him. Not surprisingly, the mission briefings for these trips supply really important insights into how Jesus intends mission to be carried out. One of these insights, which has been reflected on widely in mission thinking, is the key role that "people of peace" play in welcoming the missionary into the community. There are slightly different descriptions of the briefings for these trips in the different accounts of Jesus' life, and from these different descriptions a composite picture of what a "person of peace" looks like has been built up.

[38] Matthew 10:5-15, Mark 6:7-13, Luke 9:1-6, Luke 10:1-12

The attribute that is most often highlighted is that "people of peace" are the people who are welcoming. This idea runs through all of the accounts of these mission briefings. Its importance is expressed both positively and negatively. Its presence is to be a condition of the missionary staying in a village, and its absence should lead the missionary to leave. We have to be careful here not to universalise the applicability of instructions Jesus gave for a specific mission activity; I do not believe that this instruction should lead us to think that if we are not instantly welcomed with open arms into a community, we should abandon it. However, I do think that we should bear this facet of mission in mind. If there is really no welcome into a community at all, it will not be possible for us to be heard in it, and it is possible that God is calling us to move on to another place where we will be heard. Having said that, we also need to be aware that the way we present ourselves can make us more or less likely to be welcomed. It may not be the gospel that is being rejected, but our lack of personal hygiene. Sometimes we need to ask ourselves some hard questions and reflect on our interpersonal skills, perhaps with the support of close friends or a spiritual director. Those who are welcoming (despite our imperfections), and introduce us to others, are "people of peace".

In Luke's account of one of these mission briefings, Jesus tells his friends to accept the meals that are served to them, to stay in one house, and to receive the hospitality of the household. [39] From this instruction it can be inferred that the "people of peace" are those who serve and provide for the incomer. This can seem counterintuitive, especially if we feel that we are the ones who have something to share. Of course, there a difference between the worker being worth his wages, and greedy, simoniac profiteering from the riches of good news that God has given. Nevertheless, there is a sense in which we can only speak authentically into a community in which we are as ready to receive as we are to give. This is further illustrated by the parable of the Good Samaritan.[40] Many of us have heard this story so many times that we miss the connection between the question asked at the beginning of the story and the answer given at the end. A man is told by Jesus to love his neighbour. He asks, "Who is my neighbour?" At the end of the story

[39] Luke 10:7
[40] Luke 10:25-37

Jesus asks, "Who was neighbour to the man who was robbed?" The answer is "The one who showed him mercy" - the Samaritan. In other words, we, as the hearers of the story, are in the ditch and our neighbour is the one who serves us.[41] The person of peace is someone who serves, and we have to be willing to disclose our vulnerabilities and receive their care.

The third characteristic of "people of peace" is that they listen. This attribute is found running as a theme through these mission briefings, and is also expressed positively and negatively, often linked closely to welcome. As we discussed above, this is because welcome is a necessary precursor to listening. However, it is also important to realise that welcome does not always lead to listening. I suspect that many ministers have had the experience of being welcomed into a home with the perennial, "Tea, vicar?" and then being regaled with story after story of the exploits of grandchildren and reminiscences of times past. There is lots of welcome, but very little listening on the part of the welcomer. I might even venture to suggest that

[41] For more on this reading of this parable, and its implications, see Morisy, *Beyond the Good Samaritan* (Continuum, 2004).

in some churches a "Welcomer" badge indicates someone who is more ready to tell a visitor things than to listen to them. Some people are ready to show a deeper welcome by being open to listening to us straight away. In other situations it will be up to us to enable people to listen by responding positively to their welcome, and by being ready to listen to them first. Some people will never listen to us, but we may be unwilling to walk away from them as they are always so glad to see us. In these cases we need to exercise great discernment so that we can understand how God is calling us to focus our energies. Those who will listen are "people of peace".

I have spent some time exploring this concept and its important place in mission thinking and practice because I now believe it was a wrong understanding of this set of ideas that was forming my blinkers when I read about the King and people of Nineveh.

Knowing how important "people of peace" are in mission, in the early months of our time in Priorslee I was praying for God to show us who the "people of peace" were. I had got into my head the idea that if only I could identify them, then I could concentrate on spending time with them, and they would provide pathways into the community that would enable me to fulfil God's mission in Priorslee. Thus, when we read through Jonah, I latched onto the King of Nineveh, and identified him as a "person of peace", the one who led the rest of the community in their response to God. I spent time praying for God to show me who the "King of Nineveh" was for Priorslee - the one who would lead people in repentance. I knew that it probably wouldn't be a political leader, or even an acknowledged leader, but I was sure that there were people who were bellwethers - people who led in the community, whether they knew it or not, and who would be vitally important in the planting of a church in this area.

I do still think this is the case, but something has changed in my understanding about them. I no longer think that I need to know who they are in advance. It may be that in future I will be able to look back and discern them, but I no longer ask God to show them to me. The "people of peace" - the ones who welcomed, served and listened to Jonah first - are not named. It is they who began Nineveh's move towards repentance, but they are not discerned in advance, and are not even named in the history. In Jesus' mission briefings little is said about discerning the "people of peace" in advance.[42] The "people of peace" become apparent as the mission to their village progresses, but their identification beforehand is not specified. So, I believe, the "people of peace" in the places to which we have been sent will indeed welcome us, serve us, listen to us, and lead other people in repentance; but it is unlikely that we will know who they are in advance, or even when we first meet them.

[42] Matthew's account does record that Jesus told the disciples to "find someone worthy"; however, it seems to me that the instruction, in all the accounts, to go to a house, stay there, and to leave the village if that house was not welcoming, suggests to me that the process of "finding someone worthy" may be understood not as something to be done *before* visiting a house but as something that is accomplished *by* visiting a house.
"The "worthiness" referred to here is demonstrated, according to the following verses (cf. esp. v 14), by the receptivity shown to the disciples and their message." Hagner, *Vol. 33A: Word Biblical Commentary: Matthew 1-13*. (Word, 2002), p. 272. Reprinted by permission. All rights reserved.

To ponder:

What blinkers are you aware of when you read the Bible?

If you reflect on your life, can you discern "people of peace" who welcomed, served, and listened to you?

Did you recognise them beforehand, or afterwards?

What things that you find painful are you willing to share with others, so that they can tend your wounds?

What scars are you unwilling to let people see?

Does your welcome to people include space for them to speak?

Conversion

Human beings and animals shall be covered with sackcloth, and they shall cry mightily to God. All shall turn from their evil ways and the violence that is in their hands. (Jonah 3:8)

When we were thinking about the story of the sailors, we looked at the necessity for changed thinking to lead to changed doing as part of the process of conversion. The story of the Ninevites encourages us to think about the place that penitence has in conversion. It is clear from the story that penitence - recognising that they had done wrong and being sorry about it - was a major part of the conversion of the people of that city.

In the spring of 2012 I spent a fortnight in South Sudan, part of a team running Rooted in Jesus[43] conferences for the diocese of Nzara, in the south of the country. In what was, at the time, the newest sovereign state on earth - born of years of civil war, experiencing at first hand the evils of the Lord's Resistance Army until very recently - there was little

[43] http://www.rootedinjesus.net/

infrastructure or organised medical care, and the church had been wiped out in some places. In one exercise, exploring what the parables of the Lost Coin and the Lost Sheep can teach us about God's heart for the lost, we asked participants to think of things they had lost, and how they felt about it. Normally this exercise elicits stories of everyday lost items and the relief felt at finding them. In Nzara we heard stories of brothers and sons who had been taken off into the forest by the LRA and who had never returned, or been found dead. If there were ever people in the world who could rightly have felt themselves to be more sinned-against than sinning, it was these humble saints.

During Rooted in Jesus conferences we encourage people to share testimonies of the work God has done in their lives. At these conferences there were many stories of healing, freedom and wholeness that people had received from God. However, there was another characteristic of many of these stories that really struck me. There was an honesty and clarity about the depth of the sinfulness that people had been released from. From the woman who stood up and very calmly shared how she used to be a prostitute, but had come to faith and been forgiven and released from this slavery, to the man who detailed his alcoholism, drug dependency, and abuse of his wife before coming to know Jesus, there was a clear sight and a willingness to share how low they had been, so that they could give all the credit to God for rescuing them from these things.

One of my reflections on this was that I have rarely seen this in the church in the UK. I have rarely experienced people being willing to describe the mire that they were bogged down in when Jesus broke through into their lives. I'm not sure what the root cause of this is.

I suspect that it is a mixture of a few things. First is a tendency towards a theology of "cheap grace,"[44] in which we have so emphasised how God's grace is freely available to us that we sometimes forget how costly it was to Jesus. Second is the fact that we do not adequately consider the weightiness of sin.[45] We just do not realise how offensive our sin was and is to God.

[44] Bonhoeffer, *The Cost of Discipleship*, (Macmillan, 1966).
[45] Anselm of Canterbury, *Cur Deus homo* in McGrath, *The Christian Theology Reader* (Blackwell, 1995), p. 182.

We don't think that we were ever that bad really, and for someone to suggest that our ways were or are sinful or wicked is an unwarranted attack on our sovereign selves. Thirdly, we live in a culture that has largely done away with the concept of shame and guilt. We even have a television programme called "Shameless".

In some senses it is an age-old issue. People have rarely wanted to hear that they are sinful and need saving. We search for places to begin our conversations with people, to build relationships with them and walk with them. We show Jesus' love and live in Jesus' way to be the salt and light of the Kingdom of God in our communities. We do all these good and lovely things but, in the end, for people to be saved from the consequence of their sin - which is death - they have to repent. If they are to repent they have to recognise sinfulness. They will not be able to recognise this unless it is described and pointed out.

I wonder if the people of Nzara might be our teachers in this. I wonder if we need to get better, not at pointing out other peoples' sin, but at sharing our own sinful pasts and the story of what it feels like to be free of them. I wonder if we need to get better at humbling ourselves, saying sorry, and being penitent when we sin against others. By describing the sin in our past, and recognising the sin in our present - and dealing with them both properly - perhaps we will enable those around us to recognise their own sin and be freed from it. Part of the process of dealing with sin properly is practising acts of penitence.

Acts of penitence are about showing our sorrow for our sin. They are not done to make restitution. While it might be right for us to do all that we can to undo the harm we have done to others by our sin, we cannot undo the harm we have done to our relationship with God. There is no restitution that we can make, which is why Jesus made it for us in his death and resurrection. Acts of penitence are not done to earn or pay for our forgiveness. To repeat: this does not need to be done. Jesus has already paid our ransom and purchased our freedom.

Quite early on in their lives, my children learned to say sorry when they did something wrong. They then had to learn another lesson: that saying sorry wasn't enough. If they continued to repeatedly do something they'd been told not to do, then we stopped believing them when they said sorry. We started to teach them that they need to show that they were sorry, and not just by turning on the waterworks. If they were serious about being sorry then their behaviour had to change. They had to actually start turning their bedroom lights off when they came downstairs in the morning!

The Ninevites seemed to have understood this. They did things that showed that they were sorry, putting on the clothes of mourning. They were grieving over what they had been doing, and the consequences that Jonah had told them about. They were mourning over their deathly ways. They decided and said that they were going to change their behaviour, stop being wicked and give up violence. They were convincing enough for God to decide to forgive them and decide not to punish them (more of this conversion later).

Despite all this, and all the dramatics, it does seem that the penitence and conversion of Nineveh was short-lived. Before very long the Assyrians, and by implication the Ninevites, were up to their old tricks again. Zephaniah, some decades later, writes of how God is going to lay Nineveh waste because of its violence against God's people.[46] At a similar time, the prophet Nahum writes a book that consists almost entirely of a Judge's sentencing speech against Nineveh for its ongoing deceit, violence, and immorality. It is clear from this evidence that Nineveh as a city soon reverted to its old ways, though of course we can say nothing of the individuals involved.

I have experienced profound grief when I have seen people who have come to faith turn away from it again. Imagine how much grief was in Father's heart seeing a whole city begin to turn away again, knowing that it was a city that would go on to inflict pain and violence on others again.

It's heartbreaking, but it should not surprise us. Earlier on we thought about how Jesus described the devil as the one who comes and plucks away the seed of the good news before it can take root. In the same parable, Jesus also describes how young faith can be strangled by weeds or scorched by the sun. Jesus saw this happen in his own ministry. He saw people turn away at hard teaching, he saw his friends desert him at his hour of need, he was rejected by the people

[46] Zephaniah 2:13

from his own home town. It is important for us to remember this in all ministry, and especially in mission, for our own sanity and health. There are things that we can do to warn and protect young Christians, but in the end it is not down to us, it is down to God.

Despite these warnings, I do believe that in the end God's word is often one of promise and hope in what seem to be the darkest circumstances. Therefore, I would like to close this section on the conversion of the Ninevites with a word of hope from God's messenger, Isaiah:

> *In that day there will be a highway from Egypt to Assyria. The Assyrians will go to Egypt and the Egyptians to Assyria. The Egyptians and Assyrians will worship together. In that day Israel will be the third, along with Egypt and Assyria, a blessing on the earth. The Lord Almighty will bless them, saying, "Blessed be Egypt my people, Assyria my handiwork, and Israel my inheritance."* (Isaiah 19:23-25, NIV)

To ponder:

How do you show that you are sorry for something?

How do you feel about the prospect of sharing with a friend the details of a sin that you have been freed from?

If you have a testimony of your journey to faith does it include specific sinful behaviours that you repented of?

How do you deal with the disappointment of seeing the faith of people you have discipled being strangled or scorched?

Animals

And should I not be concerned about Nineveh, that great city, in which there are more than a hundred and twenty thousand people who do not know their right hand from their left, and also many animals?
(Jonah 4:11)

I have read, or heard read, the ending to this story in several different places and groups, and every time it has seemed odd. Odd because of its lack of resolution, and odd because of its mention of the animals. We shall explore the lack of resolution later when we discuss Jonah's conversion, or lack of it. For now our focus is on the animals.

The appearance of the animals earlier in the story is also, at first reading, a bit strange. In addition to the people putting on sackcloth and fasting, the animals were subjected to the same regime. In one group this led to some hilarity as we imagined the reaction of that household's cats to being trussed up in sackcloth - though of course, the concept of house pets would probably have been quite foreign to the people of Nineveh. The animals in question are more likely to have been the goats, sheep, and cattle that were a sign of wealth and a source of food and clothing. As such an integral part of life, and as symbols of the welfare of the city, we can begin to see why they might have been included. Although there is no direct evidence of animals being involved in mourning rites in this culture,[47] it does not take a great leap of imagination to see a parallel with the closing of shops and cessation of normal business during times of corporate mourning such as that which marked the death of Diana, Princess of Wales, in the UK.

If this were the only mention of the animals in the story, we could probably leave it at that. They would merely appear as an illustration of how deep the repentance and mourning of the people was. They were so sorry for their sinfulness that they were willing to risk their own livelihoods by not feeding their livestock during the time of the fast. It would be a culturally-specific expression of penitence that has little relevance to us. However, this is not the only

[47] "In Persian times and later, animals were sometimes made part of the mourning process (Herodotus ix.24; Plutarch, Alexander 72; Jdt 4:10) but the practice is unknown otherwise among the Assyrians." Stuart, *Vol. 31: Word Biblical Commentary: Hosea-Jonah* (Word, 2002), p. 493. Reprinted by permission. All rights reserved.

mention of the animals in the story. God mentions them as well.

Jonah is angry about the destruction of the gourd. God points out that if it is right for Jonah to be concerned about a bush, how much more right it must be for God to desire that the people and animals of Nineveh avoid destruction. By including animals in making this point, God is not saying that animals hold an equal place with humans in God's care, but that they *do* have a place in God's care, and in God's saving purposes. If this is true, it has to have implications for our mission.[48]

If this were the only evidence that animals have a place in God's care and saving purposes, then it would be a pretty feeble foundation on which to build. However, this is not the only evidence. Both of these ideas recur throughout the Biblical accounts of the Creator's interactions with creation.

God's care for animals is seen in the very first chapter of the Bible.[49] It is seen firstly in the declarations that

---

[48] See Bookless, *Planetwise* (IVP, 2008).
[49] Genesis 1

all the animals of land, sea, and air are good; that God is pleased with them. It is seen secondly in the care that God took to provide for the animals by appointing stewards – people - to look after them. It is seen thirdly in the provision of food for the animals.

God's care for animals, and their place in God's saving purposes, is seen in another story involving a lot of water and a boat: a very big boat.[50] Early in the history of creation, God is greatly saddened by the sinfulness of people, and decides that the earth must be washed clean of both people and animals. There is one man whose heart is not full of violence, Noah, and so God resolves to save him, his family, and some representative animals. God saves many more animals than humans from the flood, and then makes a covenant with both humans and animals never to flood the earth again in such a way as to destroy all living things.

When Jesus was teaching his disciples about the care that God has for them, he used several examples, based on the assumption that the Creator cares for creation. He talks about how the flowers of the field

[50] Genesis 6-9

are dressed in beautiful garments, about how the ravens are fed by God's hand, and how not even a tiny sparrow falls to the ground apart from God.[51] Jesus' point was that God cares for people even more, but the point is built on the foundation that the animals have a place in God's care.

Given this, we should recognise that the love people have for animals is part of the image of God in them. When we love animals, God has got there first. As such, this theology should be taken seriously. I have to admit that I have been a bit ambivalent about pet services and the like, but on deeper reflection I think that this ambivalence is wrong. God cares for animals, and those who love and care for their pets and other animals are being obedient to the responsibility of stewardship that God has given to all people. This obedience is worth honouring and celebrating. God cares for animals and loves to bless, so there is no reason for us to be shy about blessing animals in God's name. Doing these things is all part and parcel of God's mission to reconcile all creation to itself and to God, restoring them to the right relationships for

[51] Luke 12

which they were created.

At the beginning of our first summer in Priorslee, I was challenged to think carefully about my front lawn. This lawn has to be one the least favoured in the land. Laid on poorly-drained red clay, north-facing, it slopes away from any sun, down towards the house. Most of it is in shade, most of the time. There is significantly more moss and clover in it than grass. In addition to all this, the poor thing has been placed in the hands of a steward who hates mowing lawns: me. One day, as I was prayer-walking around the estate I found myself thanking God for all those people who obviously took good care of their front gardens and lawns and so contributed to those streets being pleasant places to walk and to live. When I arrived home from that walk and saw my poor excuse for a front garden I was convicted. How I look after this part of creation, entrusted to me, is part of my witness. It is part of the mission that God has given me here.

Raising our eyes to wider horizons, these insights might have other implications. They may have an impact on the way we make many of our shopping decisions, both individually and corporately. Often these decisions come down to a question of resources.

We want to carry out an activity and we have finite financial resources. Let us consider the example of a men's breakfast we want to host as part of a mission week in the local community. We know that we can get value eggs, bacon and sausages from the supermarket. We also know that there is a local farm shop which sells free range, organic eggs, bacon and sausages from local farmers. The first option will be a lot cheaper, and we may even be able to afford to do the event without charge. The second option will be more expensive, and may even make the whole project unachievable.

We live in a broken world, a now and not yet world, in which we cannot always make perfect decisions. With our limited knowledge and the constraints of circumstances we cannot always do all that we want to do. Nevertheless, this should not stop us seeking to do the best that we can do in any given situation. Keeping in mind God's care for creation, and our original mission as stewards of it, may challenge us severely - but embracing and rising to that challenge will bring long-lasting fruit.

To ponder:

Have you ever taken part in a service celebrating and blessing animals and their relationships with people?

Can you think of friends and neighbours who would appreciate such a service?

What animals or other parts of creation has God entrusted to your personal stewardship?

What would you have done about the men's breakfast?

Are there other things to consider from this theology in your local context?

Chapter 4

Jonah

All by Myself

Now the word of the Lord came to Jonah son of Anittai, saying, (Jonah 1:1)

When we moved to Priorslee, two local churches agreed to be our supporting churches. It was felt that some previous Pioneer Ministers in the diocese had become isolated and lonely, and that this had been destructive of their ministry. It was hoped that by providing local fellowships in which we could worship while we found our feet in the area, and who might resource the mission in Priorslee, this isolation could be avoided. This desire to create a strong support structure for us was also evident in the provisions made for line-management and supervision in the Bishop's Mission Order under which I was appointed.

We very much appreciated the support we received from these initiatives. Indeed, this book might not exist if it were not for the conversations I had in the homegroups of one of those supporting churches. The welcome, prayer support, and opportunities for friendship we have received have sustained us, especially during our first year in Priorslee.

The development of this strategy was not merely pragmatic. It has good scriptural foundations and is well-based in much contemporary thinking about mission and church leadership. Earlier we thought about the mission briefings that Jesus gave to his disciples. All of these briefings were given as Jesus sent out the disciples in pairs, rather than on their own. Almost of all Paul's missions, recorded in Acts, were carried out in mission teams, rather than as solitary endeavours.

This way of thinking also has roots in our understanding of the nature of God. We believe in one God; Father, Son, and Holy Spirit. This understanding of God puts community at the heart of our faith. There is something essentially communal about the Christian faith, a communality that is deeply rooted in our creation in the image of God.[52] Anything that is so fundamentally at the core of our faith has to inform how we go about mission, otherwise that mission will not be an authentic representation of that faith.

This understanding not only informed the support structures that were put in place for us when we moved to Priorslee, it is also the foundation of one of our key priorities. This priority is the formation and growth of a pioneer team at the core of the ministries here. Church planting and mission takes a variety of skills, abilities, and gifts. It is unlikely that one person, or even one couple, has all those gifts. God gives gifts to the people of God so that they can use them together to carry out God's work and build up the body.[53]

[52] Genesis 1:26-27
[53] Ephesians 4:11-16. Paul's primary emphasis here is on the building up of the body of Christ as currently constituted; however, I would argue that Paul would think it quite odd if this were thought not to apply to the work of mission that brings others into the body of Christ as well.

With all this in the background, it could be argued that the story of Jonah should be read as a warning against the dangers of solo ministry. The negative aspects of Jonah's journey, from the attempt to flee from the original commission all the way through to the anger and depression at the outcome of the mission, might all have been avoided or mitigated if Jonah had had co-workers. Having said that, it is a brave person who second-guesses God's purposes, and it does seem fairly clear from his individual call that God intended Jonah to go to Nineveh on his own.

In the film "Minority Report", murders are prevented by a PreCrime unit, and people are incarcerated for murders they haven't actually yet committed. The PreCrime unit is guided by visions of the future seen by three precogs, whose genetic mutation has endowed them with the ability to see the future. The film's plot, with its exploration of freewill and determinism, hinges on the fact that sometimes their visions of the future are not the same. Usually the three precogs have the same vision, but sometimes one of them sees something else – generating a minority report. This opens up the possibility that the future is still contingent, rather than determined; and this possibility provides the tension for the narrative arc of the film.[54] In courts such as the U.S. Supreme Court, which sit with more than one judge, if the judges do not agree on the verdict of the court, there may be a minority verdict written by the dissenting judge(s). Whilst this does not carry the same weight as the majority verdict in terms of legal precedent, it is an important part of the ongoing development of case law.

Rather than being a cautionary tale within the majority tradition, the story of Jonah seems to form part of a minority report within Christian scripture and tradition. This minority report is one that emphasises the isolated individual as a missionary, and provides a tension with the majority report, which describes a model of mission that is communal in shape. This minority report is one that recurs in the New Testament.

We have seen that Jesus sent out his disciples in pairs. There are also, however, examples of him sending people into the mission field on their own. On the day that Jesus stilled the storm, he and his disciples were

[54] http://www.imdb.com/title/tt0181689/

going to the country of the Gerasenes.[55] When they arrived they were met by a man whose life was also very stormy, tossed and turned by evil spirits. So Jesus calmed those storms as well, demonstrating his authority over the spiritual realm as he had just demonstrated his authority over the physical world. Having been healed, the man asked if he could go with Jesus. But Jesus said no. Instead he sent him back, on his own, to tell the people of the city what Jesus had done for him.[56]

Similarly, in the Book of Acts there are accounts of missionary activity being carried out by people on their own. The account of Philip's engagement with the Ethiopian eunuch is well known.[57] Towards the end of this episode we are told that as the two men came up out of the water following the Ethiopian's baptism, the Spirit of the Lord snatched Philip away. The Ethiopian went on, on his own, rejoicing. We do not hear of him again in Scripture, but there is a

[55] Or Gadarenes, Gergesenes, or Gergustenes. Apparently the ancient scribes really weren't very sure how you spelt the name of this place!
[56] Luke 8:26-39
[57] Acts 8:26-40

tradition that the Ethiopian church traces its roots back to his solitary witness to the people of Ethiopia. Philip landed at Azotus, and he also went on, alone, telling people about the good news of Jesus as he made his way back to Caesarea. Both men engaged in mission by themselves.

If our understanding of the Trinity places community at the heart of Christian faith and mission, then is there also a minority report about the nature of God? Because we cannot understand the mechanics of the inner workings of the Trinity it is not possible to be sure at this point. However, it does seem clear that when Jesus came to earth he did experience some kind of isolation from the other two persons of the Trinity. To become incarnate, Jesus left heaven and was, in some sense, emptied.[58] When Jesus was baptised he heard the Father speaking from heaven and the Holy Spirit was seen descending upon him.[59] It does not seem unreasonable to think therefore that one of things that Jesus was emptied of was an element of communion with the Father and Spirit. Jesus came on his mission to earth alone.

[58] Philippians 2:7
[59] Matthew 3:16-17

This minority report continues to sound all through the ages of Christian mission[60] and has important implications for how we approach the mission that we are part of today.

Firstly, it seems to suggest that becoming isolated from our own places of comfort is part of the process of dying to self, which is necessary if we are to serve those to whom we are sent. Many of the people to whom we are called to minister will feel isolated and lonely. It may be that the experience of being cut off from "people like us" is part of the softening of our hearts which makes us able to draw alongside and offer companionship to others.

Secondly, the minority report of individual sending makes clear that we are important to God individually. God knows us, loves us, calls us, and sends us as individuals. God knows your name and has prepared works for you to do. God has given each one of us specific gifts, skills, and abilities. It is our responsibility to make them available to the church and to the wider world, so that the body of Christ can

[60] For example, Donovan, *Christianity Rediscovered* (SCM, 2001) and Pullinger, *Chasing the Dragon* (Hodder and Stoughton, 2006).

be built up.

To ponder:

Do you prefer working with others or on your own?

What challenges are there in your preferred way of working?

How do you feel about the fact that God has prepared works for you to do?

When do you feel lonely?

Who do you know who may be feeling isolated?

On the move

Get up, go to Nineveh, that great city, and proclaim to it the message that I tell you. (Jonah 3:2)

God's repeated command to Jonah is as clear and direct as the first time Jonah heard it. Go to Nineveh. Jonah is to leave where he is and travel somewhere else. We've already explored some of the objections Jonah had to obeying this direction in terms of the destination, but what about the basic command, to go? What is it about going from one place to another that makes it such a big part of God's interaction with people? From Abraham, to the Exodus, to Nehemiah, to Jesus' wanderings, to Paul's missionary journeys: what is so important about *going*?

At the time of writing I am thirty-six. I have lived in at least seventeen different houses in eleven different towns or cities in three different countries. I have never lived in the same house for more than three years. The longest I have lived in the same town is seven years. You could say that I've moved around a bit. When I moved to Stoke-on-Trent I was told that folk in the Potteries tended not to move away, but to remain in close communities in the places that they were born. This was illustrated strongly for me by visits to Hanley and Burslem cemeteries, where I saw many gravestones engraved with the lifelong address of the person who had died.[61] Some people never move.

One of the frustrations of the first year of our time in Priorslee has been the challenge of recruiting a Pioneer Team to join us in mission here. Conversations with people who have a national perspective on church-planting have led us to believe that these difficulties are being experienced widely by other Pioneers and Church Planters who have been appointed by dioceses to work on suburban estates.[62]

Similar challenges are also faced by those who are recruiting people to work in Pioneer Teams in urban areas of high material deprivation. This kind of work, however, does appear to have a couple of resources that can help. The first is a very strong and simply articulated way of thinking about mission. Jesus called

[61] http://places.wishful-thinking.org.uk/STS/Burslem/ MIs.html
[62] We are particularly grateful to Bob and Mary Hopkins of Anglican Church Planting Initiatives for conversations that have sparked some of this thinking.

us to serve the poor and not to value worldly wealth. By moving from a nice middle class area to a challenging estate you can be part of bringing the Kingdom of God into that place by your presence, love, and actions. The second is the existence of high-profile visionaries who have caught hold of this imperative and who champion this type of mission work, people such as Andy Hawthorne[63] and Shane Claiborne.[64]

We do not seem to have such an easily explained way of encouraging people to move to join a Pioneer Team on a fairly well-off, middle class, suburban estate. There is the general mission imperative that Jesus came to save the world, that none may perish[65] - which would seem to suggest that we are called to take the good news of Jesus to everybody. There is a specific mission imperative based on Jesus' observation that it is easier for a camel to go through the eye of a needle than for a rich person to enter the

[63] Founder and CEO of The Message Trust.
http://www.message.org.uk/
[64] http://www.thesimpleway.org/shane/
[65] John 3:16-17

Kingdom of God[66], which implies that the rich need more help entering the Kingdom than anyone else. Even when we understand these, however, we are still faced with questions. "Why do we need to move? Why can't we just get on with the mission where we are?"

Of course, it would be ludicrous to suggest that all Christians should be moving to a new place every six months in order to engage with new opportunities for mission. In the gospels and accounts of the early church it is true that we hear a lot about people being called to come and follow, or to go and teach. We are also told a lot about missionary journeys - Paul and others travelling from one city to another to preach and plant churches. However, we have to be careful, when we read these fast-paced narratives, not to miss the half-verses, tucked in the middle of passages, which let us know that Paul stayed for significant periods of time in some places.[67] When we read carefully we discover that most of the early Christians spent most of their time staying put, though there is no doubt that it was the mobility of those who chose to travel, or who were forced to disperse by

[66] Mark 10:25
[67] e.g. Acts 18:11

persecution, that enabled the rapid spread of the Christian faith beyond Israel.

The key verse for understanding this dynamic is, as is often the case when we are thinking about mission, found at the end of Matthew's gospel, in the Great Commission.[68] Jesus' final instruction to his followers was to make disciples. As part of this instruction, Jesus mentions three actions that are going to be equally important elements of making disciples: going, baptising, and teaching.[69] That is to say, *going* is as much a part of enabling people to become wholehearted followers of Jesus as baptising and teaching are.

Two episodes from Jesus' life give us some clues as to why us going might be so indispensable in making disciples. Early in his ministry, Jesus went to the synagogue in his hometown of Nazareth and began

[68] Matthew 28:19

[69] In technical terms, 'The commission proper consists syntactically of the main verb μαθητεύσατε, "make disciples," with three parallel subordinate participles: πορευθέντες, "going," βαπτίζοντες, "baptizing," and διδάσκοντες, "teaching"' Hagner, *Vol. 33A: Word Biblical Commentary: Matthew 1-13*. (Word, 2002), p.882. Reprinted by permission. All rights reserved.

teaching. But the people there would not listen to him. They could not see beyond their experiences of him as a lad growing up, or past the fact that some of them were married to his sisters, or that last summer he'd been the chippy on the local building sites. [70] Sometimes our own history with people can stop them hearing what we have to share about Jesus.

We have already seen how Jesus experienced a kind of dislocation when he left heaven to come to earth. It was costly to him. On one occasion he was talking to some people who wanted to follow him about the costs that they would incur if they decided to do so. He contrasts himself with wild animals who at least have dens to hide in, and to birds who have nests to settle in. But he is so far from home that he doesn't even have a place to lay his head.[71]

In the same way that isolation can equip us to come alongside those who are isolated, so having experienced dislocation can help us in our understanding of what it takes for someone to come to faith. This is particularly true for those of us who

[70] Luke 4:16-30
[71] Luke 9:57-62

were brought up in Christian homes and have had a Christian faith for as long as we can remember. We have never experienced the dislocation that coming to faith can cause for some people. One way of thinking about becoming a Christian is to see it as moving home. You leave the world and move to the house of God.[72] The angels rejoice, but the person moving may also be grieving for the things and people that they are leaving behind.

In "The Pilgrim's Progress," John Bunyan describes a dream of a journey taken by a man, Christian, through life.[73] The story begins with Christian reading a book and realising that the city where he lives is going to be destroyed, and that he needs to leave if he is to live. He tries to tell his friends and family but they will not listen: in fact they think he's gone mad. In the end he makes a run for it, on the advice of Evangelist, and begins his journey towards the place of safety, the Celestial City. In doing so he has to stop his ears and yell so that he cannot hear the cries of his wife and children calling him back. People coming to faith can

[72] Ephesians 2:18-20
[73] Bunyan, *The Pilgrim's Progress* (Oxford University Press Reissue Edition, 2008).

experience profound dislocation, and it may be important for us to experience that kind of dislocation and relocation in order to walk with them as they experience it.

Having said all this, in the end it comes down to us being open to hear and ready to obey what God is saying to us about where we are to join in God's mission. For Jonah it was an instruction to go to Nineveh, leaving the place where he was known as a prophet and had stature and a public profile.

We live in a fairly mobile society. People move for jobs, so that their children can go to a certain school, to be near family, and so that they can live in a nice place. Are we willing to be open to the possibility that God might be instructing us to move for the far greater purpose of helping people come home to God?

To ponder:

Where is (or was) Nineveh for you?

When did you last ask God where you are to go?

Do you have a history in the place where you live that is a barrier to mission?

Are you deeply rooted or easily transplanted?

When in your life have you felt most dislocated?

Where do you feel most at home?

Telling it how it is

Jonah began to go into the city, going a day's walk. And he cried out, 'Forty days more, and Nineveh shall be overthrown! (Jonah 3:4)

Jonah really did not want to deliver this message. He went to great lengths to avoid sharing it. When he did get round to it, he didn't worry about building relationship bridges with people, or serving the community, or building up social capital. He just wandered in and started shouting from the street corners and in the marketplaces that in forty days the city would be overthrown. Jonah had a very strong reason for not wanting to deliver this message: he didn't want it to be effective. However, in the end, he was obedient to God and he did deliver it, and it did have an effect.

When I reflect on how I would have responded to God's instruction to take this message, I don't think I would have wanted to deliver it either. Not because I wouldn't have wanted it to be effective, but because it seems to be the kind of message that would be likely to get me lynched or, in a best-case scenario, laughed at. Telling people that their way of life is one that will lead to their destruction - that judgement is coming and that their society is doomed - does not feel like a very comfortable thing to have to say. It doesn't feel like good news. I really would not want to do it. In fact, I would be much happier getting on a boat to Tarshish.

God's instruction to Jonah was unambiguous. God told him what to say, and (as far as we know) Jonah went and said it. What about us, today? Is there a similarly direct, but also uncomfortable, message that we have been given to share with the world?

There is a very clear call to repentance running all the way through the New Testament. One of the interesting things about it is the number of times it appears in reported speech. Again and again we hear preachers telling their hearers that they need to repent. Even before Jesus starts his ministry, we find his cousin, John, in the wild places calling the people of God to repent.[74] When Jesus does start his public ministry, it is also, in summary, a call to repent.[75] When Jesus sent his followers out on their mission field trip, they also preached the need for people to

[74] Matthew 3:2
[75] Matthew 4:17

repent.[76] After Jesus had finished his earthly ministry and returned to heaven, his followers gathered in Jerusalem, as he had told them to. One morning, during the harvest festival known as Pentecost, they were empowered by the Holy Spirit to start preaching, so they did. The climax and punchline of that preaching, delivered by Peter, was a call to repentance.[77] In the philosophers' debating circle in Athens, Paul preached that God is calling people everywhere to repent.[78] The theme continues right through to the end of the Bible. In John's account of the vision he was given of heaven, we hear Jesus speaking from his throne to seven churches. Even here the message to some of them is that they need to repent.[79]

It is an unavoidable conclusion that a call to repentance is a non-negotiable element of how we are to communicate the good news of Jesus. The fact that this is a hard message to share is demonstrated by the fate of the people who have delivered it. John was

[76] Mark 6:12
[77] Acts 2:38
[78] Acts 17:30
[79] Revelation 3:19

imprisoned and beheaded, largely because of his call to King Herod to repent. Jesus was crucified. Peter was probably crucified, and crucified upside down at that. Paul was probably beheaded. According to the traditions of the early church, ten out of the original twelve apostles were martyred. Calling people to repent is likely to be costly to us. However, there are a variety of ways in which a message can be delivered.

In the Stella Gibbon's comic novel we meet Amos Starkadder, who preaches weekly at the Church of the Quivering Brethren. The meetings of this sect, the hymns (including the conductor's fire poker baton, reminding the Brethren of the fires of hell), the prayers, and the preaching, all focus entirely on the sinfulness of the world and the torments of hell that await the Brethren. As Amos puts it when describing his sermon preparation, "I allus knows 'twill be summat about burnin' ... or the eternal torment ... or sinners comin' to judgement."[80]

We might not want to model the way that we call people to repent on Amos. He seems to have missed the point that a call to repentance is part of the *good*

<hr>

[80] Gibbons, *Cold Comfort Farm* (Penguin, 1938), p. 89ff.

news of Jesus.

Tony Campolo writes about the practical implications of living out a Christian faith in a postmodern Western context. He explores different aspects of life and encourages us to think wisely about how we can follow Jesus faithfully without doing damage to God's reputation. However, in the final chapter, he acknowledges that sometimes we are called to do things that are foolish in the eyes of the world. To illustrate this point he gives examples of people sharing the good news of Jesus in ways which might seem foolish or even dishonouring to God, but which were fruitful. He tells the story of a time when he was walking along a beachfront with his wife and saw a barefoot street preacher, with open Bible, pointing at people, calling out, "Woe unto you...". Campolo was indignant about the negative impact this would have on peoples' perception of God, and muttered darkly to his wife. Some time later, as they completed the return leg of their stroll, they came across the preacher again. This time he had two men with him, wearing business suits. He had his arms around them in prayer as they responded to Jesus' call on their lives.[81]

Sometimes we will be called to say hard things to people, and we may be led to foolish ways of saying them. As we say these things we must do so with humility, gentleness, and love. We are not excused from doing all that we can to present the message we have been given in a way that will maximise the likelihood of it being heard. Discerning how we should do this requires us to be sensitive to the guidance and direction of the Holy Spirit. At the heart of this is the fundamental understanding that repentance brings freedom, that the call to repent is good news, and that we are not about making people feel worse, but about giving them hope.

There seem to be two dynamics at work in the prevailing culture at the moment. The first is one which has convinced people that they are not good enough. The relentless communication through every media stream of the perfect ideals of beauty, form, and wealth has set the bar so high that many people feel that they are lacking. This is especially true for

[81] Campolo, *Following Jesus without Embarrassing God* (Word, 1997), p. 271ff.

those trapped in poverty and worklessness. The symptoms of this dynamic are seen in the increase of self-harming behaviours in our young people, in the rise in cosmetic surgeries, and in the growth of household debt and consumer credit. The second dynamic is one that comes out of a postmodern belief in the inalienable right of each person to define their own truth and right; to tell their own story. Perhaps in part as a self-defence against the harm of the first dynamic, people are choosing a way of seeing themselves that is positive, with little or no reference to external perspectives. This can be seen graphically exposed in the cruel parade of contestants who believe that they have a singing talent on programmes such as "The X-Factor".

These dynamics have to inform how we present the call to repent. The call to repent asserts that there is an external perspective - God's – and that is absolute. From this perspective, we have all fallen short of what we were created for. We have all turned away from the one who created us and loves us. We have all chosen to live on our own terms. We have all sinned. And we need to repent. However, this is not everything that can be said about God's perspective.

This is the perspective that is trustworthy, because it is absolute. It is this perspective which says we are worth so much to God that Jesus came to live among us and die for us. It is the perspective that saw us in our mother's womb, that formed us, and that longs for us to be redeemed children in God's family.

The call to repent is not one that is easy to share. It is likely that it will make us unpopular. However, it is good news for those who hear and receive it. Our willingness to share it is a measure of the depth of our love for the people that we are sent to, and of our obedience to God. It has the power to release people into the knowledge of who they can be: the sons and daughters of God.

To ponder:

Who called you to repent?

How did they do it?

Do you recognise the two dynamics of a lack of self-worth and of self-defence at work in your friends, neighbours, or work colleagues?

Which one is dominant?

What would repentance mean for these people?

How do you feel about calling people to repent?

How does that make you feel?

But God said to Jonah, 'Is it right for you to be angry about the bush?' And he said, 'Yes, angry enough to die.'
(Jonah 4:9)

Jonah's inner life really is a mess. His emotions are dark and his feelings overwhelm him. There are three emotions in particular that we can see expressed in this story: despair, anger, and grief. These three emotions have a huge impact on how Jonah approaches his mission, and can have a similar negative impact on our effectiveness in mission if we do not recognise them and seek God's healing for them.

The first indication we have of Jonah's tendency to despair is in his response to the sailors on the boat. Having ascertained that he is the cause of the trouble they are in, they ask him what they should do about it. There is no suggestion that Jonah asks God for guidance, he just tells them to throw him overboard.[82] No hint of returning him to Joppa, or diverting to Nineveh, both of which would have indicated to God

[82] Jonah 1:12

that Jonah was going to do as he had been commanded. No, Jonah was going to keep running away, even if that meant his death. He would rather die than do what God had told him to do. There is despair here, a rejection of any hope for a way out, and an embrace of victimhood that is deeply unhealthy and ultimately life-threatening. These can be seen surfacing in Jonah's heart at the end of the story. He would rather die than return home and tell his friends and fellow citizens that he has been part of bringing salvation to Nineveh. He does not want to continue living if this is what living looks like. He is in despair.[83]

When I was at university I took up rowing. I was never particularly good, but I competed at a level which meant that I was expected to show a reasonable level of commitment to training. I enjoyed it, but particularly towards the end of my course, as exams loomed, I became less sure that I could justify the time I was giving to it. Whenever things went

[83] Samaritans exist to support those who are experiencing feelings of despair, including those which may lead to suicide. They can be contacted in the UK on 08457 90 90 90 or by email jo@samaritans.org.

badly in training, or we lost a race, I would have a nagging voice at the back of my mind: "You're like Jonah to this crew. It's going badly because you shouldn't be there. It's all your fault."

I have had to battle this internal script in many different situations through my life. It is an irrational, life-sapping script of despair, and it is life-threatening. When I fail in my roles as husband or father, the script runs: "You're like Jonah to this family. You should never have got married or had children, what did you think you were doing?" When things go wrong in ministry the script runs: "You're like Jonah to this project. Whatever made you think you were called to this? You're never going to succeed." The despair seeps in and the temptation increases to jack it all in, to give up, to choose not to live the life I have been given and called to.

We have each been given resources to help us in this battle. We do not have to listen to this kind of script. It is not from God, it is a tissue of lies about who we are and about who God is. If we have been disobedient, as Jonah was, it may be that the difficulties we're facing are a consequence of our disobedience. In that case, we are not called to despair but to repentance, and to the freedom that is ours through repentance. If we are doing what God has called us to do, then we can rest secure in that. The success or failure of what we are doing is not ultimately our responsibility. It is God's. It really is not about us. Our fundamental worth and loveliness are not rooted in who we are or what we do; they are rooted in who God is and what God has done.[84] This truth gives us hope and life.

The second emotion we encounter with Jonah is his anger. We've already explored some of the external factors that might have made Jonah angry that God had saved the people of Nineveh. What about the internal factors? What might have been going on in his heart?

Jesus told a story that might help us to explore this. He spoke of a landowner who had a vineyard.[85] There was work to be done in the vineyard, so he went down to the marketplace early in the morning and hired some workers, agreeing to pay them a full day's wage. A few hours later he returned to the hiring area and saw some more potential workers waiting around. He

[84] On this theme, I love the song "Who am I" by Casting Crowns
[85] Matthew 20:1-16

hired them as well, agreeing to pay what was right. He returned three more times, including a last time at five o'clock. Each time he hired more workers, agreeing to pay them what was right. At the end of the day he gathered the workers together to pay them. He paid them in reverse order, giving those he had hired last a full day's wage. Those who had been hired first started to get their hopes up, but when it was their turn they also were paid a full day's wage. They were angry at this perceived injustice: they'd done most of the work, and had been paid the same as those slackers who had turned up for a couple of hours at the end of the day. They grumbled. The landowner answered them, saying that they had been paid fairly, and that his generosity to others did not make his treatment of them unjust.

Is Jonah angry because he believes that God's generosity to the people of Nineveh is unjust and unfair compared to the long faithfulness of God's people, the Israelites? We don't know for certain, but it seems reasonable to think that this might have been part of it. Whether or not Jonah was angry for this reason, it is good for us to guard against this kind of anger and bitterness. When we have been working long hours in the heat of the sun, when the earth has been hard and the toil exhausting, when the battles have been hard and we are wounded and bleeding., it can be tempting to be jealous of those who seem to have an easier road to walk, who come to faith and encounter blessing that we feel that we can only dream of. Let us not be like Jonah, robbed of the sweet taste of seeing salvation come by the bitterness of our own anger.

The third emotion that Jonah expresses is grief. He grieves over the plant that God provided to give him shelter, which has now died. God does not say that Jonah is wrong to grieve for the plant, but God does invite Jonah to consider whether or not there might have been more important things for him to grieve over, such as the hundred and twenty thousand inhabitants of Nineveh (and not forgetting the animals). In fact, God provides shelter, and then withdraws that provision in order to make this point to Jonah.

God continues to issue this invitation to the church today. There is a sense in which many of the forms of church life that have sheltered us in the past are dying or have died. This process is quite naturally leading us to grief. There has been loss, and we feel bereft. Many feel that they are losing shelter, and feel exposed and threatened. This grief is understandable, but God's challenge remains. Is there something more important to be grieving over, to be concerned about? In our situation there are about four and a half thousand people living in Priorslee, about one hundred and seventy thousand living in Telford, and about sixty-three million in the UK. The vast majority of these do not know their right hand from their left, so to speak. It is these whom God is heartbroken over, and we are invited into that concern and grief over the lives that are being lost.

Jonah's inner life really is a mess. By contrast, this brief exploration of the damaging emotions that he was experiencing has been very neat. We've taken each of three emotions in turn. We've looked at the causes of these emotions, their impacts, and some possible remedies, but in reality our emotional lives are never neat. Anger, despair, and grief tangle together, overlap, and feed each other. They cannot be contained by neat strategies; they sneak out and creep up on us again. The positive side of this is that other emotions work the same way. Love, hope, and peace also weave together, reinforce and nourish each other. They overflow and bear us up at the least expected moment. By God's grace and generosity we can have emotional lives that are healthy and life-giving, and are a fountain of living water to those around us.

To ponder:

Do you recognise these scripts of despair, or are there other negative scripts that run through your mind from time to time?

What other story told by Jesus illustrates the problem of jealousy towards those who have experienced the generosity of God?

How can we discern what is breaking God's heart, and are we heart broken by the same things?

In our time, is God withdrawing the provision of shelter for God's people in order to provoke us to consider what is really important to us?

Conversion?

And now, O Lord, please take my life from me, for it is better for me to die than to live. (Jonah 4:3)

We have already seen how many of the characters in this story experienced a conversion - a change of direction and life. The sailors and people of Nineveh for sure. The fish (perhaps). Later we will think about God's conversion. One character stands out, though, as remaining unconverted: Jonah. Now, it could be argued that his song of praise in the belly of the fish, and his change of mind about going to Nineveh indicate that he was converted to God's way of thinking. However, the last part of the story and the strength of his negative feelings towards God and the people of Nineveh show that Jonah's heart had not changed. Indeed, his thanksgiving for his own deliverance from destruction, expressed in that central psalm, throws into contrast his anger over the deliverance from destruction experienced by the people of Nineveh.[86] Jonah ends the story, as he began, estranged in his heart from God's heart.

[86] Stuart, *Vol. 31: Word Biblical Commentary: Hosea-Jonah* (Word, 2002), p. 439. Reprinted by permission. All rights reserved.

One of the counter-intuitive aspects of this is that this doesn't seem to have reduced Jonah's missional effectiveness. We have just been reminded that through his ministry both the sailors and the people of Nineveh were converted. Based on a count of the number of people turning towards God, Jonah was a successful missionary. A very real temptation in the arena of mission is to draw too close a connection between our own standing before God and the apparent success of the work we are doing. For the sake of our own spiritual health we should remember that the fact that we are seeing people come to faith through our ministries does not mean that our hearts are beating in time with God's heart. Conversely, it is also true to say that we should not always assume that the apparent failure of a mission initiative is down to our sinfulness, lack of faithfulness, or inability to hear God rightly. There is a connection between our faithfulness and our fruitfulness, but it is less clear-cut than we might think, and the fruit might only be visible from the perspective of eternity.

Another thing that might puzzle us is what it means to say that one of God's people still needs to be converted. Jonah was one of God's people. More than

Jonah

that, he was a prophet to God's people, entrusted by God with speaking God's word with authority and power. He worshipped God, he heard God speaking, he prayed and conversed with God. How could such a person need to be converted?

When we start to think about how this might apply to our own lives and mission, our puzzlement might only increase. We live in a different age. We have seen Jesus live among us, die for us, and be raised to heaven. As a result of that, the way has been opened for us to become children of God, a new creation, with the past put behind us and forgiven. We have been changed - converted - and there is no going back. Of course, we know that we are not yet perfect. The daily evidence of our lives shows that we still sin and fall short of God's perfection. We are aware that as we follow Jesus' way the Holy Spirit is at work in us, making us more and more able to walk that way without stumbling. We sometimes describe this as sanctification, becoming holy, purification, or refining as silver is refined. But what about conversion? Is it helpful or accurate to use this word to describe something that people of God still need to experience?

Jesus told a story about a man who found a treasure

143

buried in a field. The man reburied the treasure, went and sold all that he had and then returned to buy the field that contained the treasure.[87] This parable provides a framework to Gerard Hughes' exploration of how we understand ourselves. He suggests that as we dig in the field that is ourselves, searching for the treasure of the Kingdom, we find that "there are layers upon layers of consciousness within us and on our journey towards God we are constantly discovering areas of atheism within us, provided we dare look."[88] This describes very clearly how I have felt at times when circumstances or particular events have broken through a door or a floor in my life and revealed to me a whole area of my life that is, effectively, Godless. I could use the language of sanctification to describe what needs to happen in these areas of my life, but the language of conversion feels more realistic.

One of the things that can break through those floors and doors, revealing areas of our lives that need converting, is the experience of reaching out to others.

[87] Matthew 13:44

[88] Hughes, *God of Surprises* (Darton, Longman and Todd, 2008), p. 66.

It may be that part of God's purpose in sending Jonah to Nineveh was to reveal to Jonah a part of his life that needed to be converted.

At one stage in his wanderings around the Palestinian countryside, Jesus decides to take a break and escape from the public demands of ministry in seaside town of Tyre. While he's there a woman comes to see him and asks him to free her daughter from an unclean spirit. But there's a problem. The woman isn't Jewish; she's a foreigner and a gentile. So Jesus tells her that it would be wrong to give the children's food to the dogs before the children have had their fill. The woman is graceful in humility, answering that even the dogs under the table get the food falling from the children's plates. At this Jesus changes his mind and tells the woman that her daughter is freed from the unclean spirit. Jesus then goes on to continue ministering in gentile areas of the country, healing the sick and feeding the hungry.[89]

Jesus was open to the possibility that his understanding of his own mission could be shaped and changed by someone who was outside his own

[89] Mark 7:24ff

faith community. Whilst I do hesitate to suggest that Jesus was converted from a hardness of heart that might indicate him having sinned, I think that it is reasonable to say, at least, that Jesus' appreciation of the breadth and extent of his Father's love and purpose was widened in this encounter. Given that this was the case for Jesus, how much more should we be open to the possibility that the mission God has called us to engage in might be as much about deepening our conversion as it is about converting others?

This openness does not just apply to us as individuals, but also corporately; as local churches and as a national institution. I am writing this in late November 2012. It is the day after the General Synod of the Church of England voted down proposed legislation that would have allowed the ordination of women as bishops in the Church of England. There were many threads in this debate, but there was one that struck me as particularly relevant here, about the place that the opinion of those outside of the Church should have in the Church's decision-making. Some argued that the Church should be distinct from the world, and if she feels she is right about something then she should stick to it, however much the world disapproves or fails to understand. Others argued that in this case the surrounding culture is more Christlike than the Church and is showing the Church a better way. Failing to walk in that way would create such an offence that we would less likely to be heard when we suggest that following Jesus might be good news.

In his letter to the people of God in Rome, Paul writes, "Do not conform to the pattern of this world, but be transformed by the renewal of your mind. Then you will be able to test and approve what God's will is – God's good, pleasing, and perfect will."[90] This is a verse I have returned to repeatedly - or which has returned to me - throughout my life. I believe that it can help us to resolve this tension. We are called to be distinct from the world and from our surrounding culture and its normal patterns of life, where they are unhealthy and life-destroying. However, we have to remain open to the possibility that the world might be one of God's agencies in the work of renewing our minds. If we, as individuals and as a community of faith, are closed to this possibility, then our mission to

[90] Romans 12:2

others might be successful but we run the risk of ending up sat next to Jonah, with our hearts estranged from God's heart, longing for death. Alternatively, we might choose to join Brueggemann in his prayer:

> Enter the deep places of our life and claim us for your purposes.
> We would be more free than we are,
> more bold than we dare,
> more obedient than we choose."[91]

To ponder:

How would you describe your conversion to Christ?

How would you measure the success of a mission?

Can you think of a time where your understanding of God was deepened by a conversation with someone who is not a Christian?

How do you feel about the idea that there might be areas of your life that are Godless?

Is there a place of darkness in your heart that the Holy Spirit is prompting you to expose to Christ's light today?

---

[91] Brueggemann, *Prayers for a Privileged People* (Abingdon, 2008), p. 30. Used with permission.

Jesus

...but emptied himself, taking the form of a slave, being born in human likeness. And being found in human form, he humbled himself and became obedient to the point of death – even death on a cross.
(Philippians 2:7-8)

Jesus and Jonah; both men sent by God. Both with a challenging message for a tough audience. Both sent far from home. But what a contrast in attitude and heart. Jonah ran away from the mission that God had for him. Jesus embraced his mission wholeheartedly. Jonah remained hard-hearted and full of himself. He kept himself apart and separate. Jesus emptied himself and was full of compassion. He joined in the life of the community to which he had been sent.

We are people sent by God, we have a challenging message for a tough audience, we live far from our eternal home, and we have decisions to make about how we are going to react to these realities. It is not enough for us to say that we want to follow the example of Jesus and avoid the mistakes that Jonah made. We have to do the work of engaging with what that might actually mean in reality. Paul's description, in his letter to the church at Philippi, of what Jesus did when he came to earth, can give us a framework to engage with these realities.

Jesus emptied himself. If we are to follow in Jesus' way then we too will have to become emptier. Sometimes this will be a voluntary emptying, as Jesus' was, and sometimes we may find circumstances have emptied us and we only realise when we feel the loss associated with it.

We have already talked about emptying ourselves of sin and receiving forgiveness that frees us to live authentic lives for Jesus. In addition to this kind of emptying, there might also be things in our lives that are not wrong, and might even be good, but which need to go in order to make space for new things. For instance, in order to make time and space for the development of new friendships we might need to let go of existing ones. In order to make room for hospitality to others we might need to let go of some of our privacy and our desire to shut the world out of our safe spaces. In order to be able to engage fully in community life we might need to give up a pastime or hobby that we have found fulfilling and life-sustaining.

When I moved to Priorslee, there was a sense in which I was forcibly emptied by the context. I hadn't been a full-time minister for very long, just for three years of a training curacy. Even in that time, however, I had become accustomed to some of the fullness of an inherited way of doing church and ministry. In the early days of the type of church plant we are embarking on, there are very few resources to hand. There is no building, there are few people, we are strangers. Everything we do depends on the generosity and hospitality of other people.[92] This is a vulnerable place to be. It empties us of self-reliance, power, and control. I feel empty, but hold on to the fact that this emptiness is one that God is looking to fill with a new way of being, one that is more dependent on God and less dependent on treasures stored up on earth.

In his great hymn, Wesley writes that Jesus "emptied himself of all but love".[93] The risk of emptying is that we shrink and become hard-hearted, and our capacity

---

[92] I am grateful to Steve Kelly, a fellow church planter, for the insights that allowed me to name this dynamic, which had been affecting me without me being able to identify it.
[93] Wesley, *And Can it Be* 1738

to love is reduced. This would be disastrous to our own souls, never mind our mission.

Jesus took the form of a slave. More than that, he took on the duties of slave, most famously on his last night with his friends.

He washed their feet. Their dusty, grimy, walked-in-the-heat-of-the-day feet. He washed them and commanded them to serve each other in the same way.[94] Serving others was at the heart of Jesus' mission, and is also at the heart of our mission. This is not only the case for people's felt or apparent needs, but also for their visions. The Head of your local school may have a vision for that school. The medical practice round the corner may have a vision for their service to the community. The residents' association may have ideas about how they want the local area to develop. It may be that part of our mission is to serve these visions, as well as the people who have them. These visions may not be consciously identified or described as vision - such language may be completely foreign to the context we have been sent to. Sometimes the beginning of serving this vision is

[94] John 13:1-17

listening for it in the heartfelt longings of the people, and helping them to see that the future can look different.

Jesus humbled himself. In some senses, this repeats what we have already heard. Jesus leaves his place of glory and privilege and takes a lower place in the order of things. In fact, he goes from the highest place, that of God the rightful owner of all, to the lowest place, that of a slave: beholden to others and owner of nothing. However, it does add another dimension to this movement, the dimension of one's attitude towards others. As Paul writes a little earlier in this letter, "in humility, value others above yourselves."[95] This understanding of what humility means is echoed in Paul's letter to the church in Rome, to whom he writes, "Honour one another above yourselves."[96]

We have already seen how Jesus put this into practice in his service of his friends. Countless further examples can be found in the times that Jesus was looking for rest, but found people in need and ministered to them instead; in the times that he

[95] Philippians 2:3b
[96] Romans 12:10b, NIV

reached out to those on the edges of society, those with leprosy, widows, tax collectors, prostitutes, and demonstrated by his willingness to touch them and be seen with them that they were valuable to him. They were more valuable to him than his reputation was, more valuable than his safety or his social standing. He honoured them above himself.

C.S. Lewis' Screwtape, giving devilish advice, describes Spiritual Pride as "the strongest and most beautiful of vices."[97] The idea that we are in some way superior to those to whom we are sent is dangerous to our own souls and fatal to our mission. We must hold on to the fact that we have been saved by grace: by God's goodness and love, freely given. We do not deserve it and have not earned it. Any progress we have made towards living a godly life is entirely down to the work of the Holy Spirit in us. We have as much business being proud of it as we have being proud of the colour of our hair. We need to hold on to the fact that we are not the Messiah, we are very naughty boys.[98]

[97] Lewis, *The Screwtape Letters* (Fount, 1977), p.122.
[98] With apologies to the Monty Python crew for the misquote

Jesus was obedient. We have already thought about the necessity for us to obey when we are sent, and to be obedient to the call that God has put on our lives to engage in mission. There is a sense, however, in which these, and other, obediences flow out of the greatest obedience. The greatest obedience is that which is obedient to the greatest commands. According to Jesus the greatest commands are to love God with all our heart and mind and soul, and to love our neighbours as ourselves.[99]

As God peels back the layers of Jonah's disobedience, the heart of the matter is exposed: the disobedience at the core of all Jonah's disobedience, which is to one (if not both) of the heart commandments. It seems quite clear from the narrative that Jonah did not love the Ninevites. He might have argued that they were not his neighbours but his enemies, and therefore were not within the scope of the command. We, however, have no such excuse. Jesus, in telling the story of the good Samaritan[100], clearly defines all people as our neighbours, including our enemies. Obeying this command is beyond me. It only becomes possible for

[99] Matthew 22:36
[100] Luke 10:25-37

me as I learn to live in the reality of the love that God has for me. It is God's love that holds me so securely that I can risk loving God back and risk loving others in the same way.

To ponder:

Are there areas of your life that feel empty, or that need to be emptied?

Do you have a sense of what God might be preparing for those voids?

Whose vision are you serving?

Are there other people in your community who you might be able to come alongside in making a new vision come to fruition?

Which of your neighbours do you find least loveable?

What is your experience of expressing and talking about loving God?

Chapter 5

God

Which God?

*'I am a Hebrew,' he replied. 'I worship the LORD, the
God of heaven, who made the sea and the dry land.'*
(Jonah 1:9)

I wonder when you last read the translators' preface
at the beginning of your Bible. Most modern
translations have one, and as well as telling you who
did the translation, the sources they worked from, and
the methods they used, there is usually a note about
the way that they have chosen to deal with the name
of God. This name is represented in Old Testament
Hebrew by four consonants - YHWH - which were

157

written in early English translations as "Jehovah."[101]
More modern translations, taking seriously the Jewish
belief that this name should not be written in full,
often represent it as "LORD". The normal word for
God, "elohim", is translated as "God" or "god" and the
usual word for Lord, "adonai", is written as "Lord".

All three of these words appear in different places in
the story of Jonah.[102] Whilst the pattern is not
concrete, it does seem as though, in general, Jonah
uses the specific name of God that had been given to
the people of God.[103] In contrast, the sailors and the
Ninevites use the more general word for God. This can
be seen in the conversation that Jonah has with the
sailors during the storm. The sailors are praying to
their gods, and they ask Jonah to call on his god. They
cast lots and, when the lot falls on Jonah, they ask him
lots of questions, at which point he shares God's name
with them. In their later prayers, the sailors start to
use the name for God that they have been given.

[101] It is likely that Yahweh is a more accurate pronunciation than
Jehovah.
[102] You might want to take a few minutes now to go through the
story of Jonah in a translation that makes these distinctions clear
and note when the different words are used.
[103] Exodus 3

Names are really important, because they are bound up with identity and with our understanding of ourselves and of what things are. This importance is grasped from a very early age. When children are upset by unkind things that someone has said to them, they will often describe it as "being called names." They sense that their identity is under attack. What is slightly strange about this is that few of us get to choose our personal names, but most of us learn to identify ourselves with our names.

Recently we bought a hamster. When we got it home, one of the first things that had to be done was to give it a name. We had a democratic process, in which each member of the family chose a name, all four of which were voted on via a complicated system of transferable votes. In the end the name "Bilbo" was chosen. This naming was informed by the upcoming cinema release of a film of "The Hobbit", by the cuteness of the hamster, and the similarities between the diminutive size, and the eating and sleeping habits, of both hobbits and hamsters. So, the hamster was named.

When I meet a person for the first time, they will usually tell me their name. I cannot decide that they look like a hobbit and therefore I am going to call them Bilbo. They already have a name, one that has been given to them or which they have chosen, and they have decided to share it with me. Although, in the western culture of informality, we seem to have little choice about who we share our names with. We're on first name terms with almost everyone. This has not always been in the case, and isn't the norm in many other cultural contexts, where personal names are closely guarded and shared only with close friends and family.

What is really important about the name of God that Jonah shares with the sailors is that it is not a name that God had been given by people, but one that was revealed to God's people by God himself. God is unique, in that God is not named by humans. Everything else that we speak of has been named by a human being. God is different. God chooses a name, one that tells us something about who God is. God also chooses to share that name with people, a decision that tells us something else about what God is like. The fact that God has shared God's name with people shows that God is knowable to some extent, and wants to be known. Jonah, however, does not just share God's name with the sailors, but also some of the attributes of God. Particularly, he says that God is the one who made the sea and the dry land.

This one sentence of Jonah's has massive implications. There is a God who has a name that was not given by people to God but by God to people. This God is knowable and wants to be known. Knowing God and accepting God's exclusive claim means rejecting other understandings of deity.

There is a similar dynamic at work in a speech which Paul made in Athens.[104] Having spent some time wandering around the city and speaking at various public gatherings, Paul is invited to speak to the local philosophers' guild. He begins his speech by sharing an observation he had made on his wanderings, that there was a place of worship in Athens dedicated to an unknown god. He goes on to argue that what the Athenians thought was unknown is actually knowable: the God who created everything and who is Lord of all. Paul is clear that accepting these claims would mean the Athenians giving up their current beliefs about the gods: they would have to stop worshipping idols

[104] Acts 17:22-29

made by people.

As the representatives of God in our homes, workplaces, schools, and clubs we are in a similar place to Jonah and to Paul. We will meet people who have many different beliefs about god(s). Some will believe that there is no god. Some will believe in god, but may have difficulty in talking about what they mean by that. Others believe in a god that bears little or no resemblance to God. With all these people, we are called to share what God has shown us, God's name and God's desire to be known.

With those who do not believe in any god, it may be interesting to ask them to describe the god that they don't believe in. It may be that you don't believe in that god either, and that that common ground can be a useful starting point for further conversations about faith and God. With those who believe in a god, it can also be helpful to explore what they mean by that. Is what they believe in personal or impersonal? Do they know its name? Does the god they believe in make claims on their lives? What difference does believing in that god make to the way in which they live their lives?[105]

When we come across ideas of god that are contrary to what God has revealed, we need to have the confidence and boldness to say so. I sometimes find that I am so concerned to avoid coming across as arrogant or dogmatic that I fail to speak the truth. Christianity is not merely a set of truths or beliefs about God on which we all have to agree. It is much more than that, but I would argue that it does include that. God is beyond our complete understanding and knowledge, but there are things that we can know about God, because they have been revealed to us. God is the creator of all. God is love. God is Father, Son, Spirit. God is the redeemer. God makes claims on our lives, and our response to those claims is important. We should be respectful and courteous in sharing what we believe to be true, but we must still do it. This is particularly important given the prevalence of negative images and ideas about God that surround us. Laurence Singlehurst suggests that given this, one of our first steps in evangelism is helping people to see

---

[105] See Fincher & Fincher, *Coffee Shop Conversations* (Zondervan, 2010), Chapter 12 for a more thorough exploration of these ideas.

that God is good.[106]

This does, of course, assume that we know what we are talking about. Another reason that we might avoid talking about God, and about what God is like, is that we're not sure ourselves. In his letters to Timothy, his apprentice, Paul repeatedly tells him to watch his doctrine, to hold on to sound teaching and to get his thinking straight. This is part of the work that we are called to as followers of Jesus; both for our own sakes and for the sake of those to whom we are sent. It is not always easy work; God is big, and our minds and hearts are small. However, we should be encouraged that God has taken the first steps towards us by sharing God's name and inviting us to get to know God better. Jesus showed us what God is like, and the Holy Spirit continues the work of teaching and guiding us as we read the Bible, pray, and spend time with God and with others who know God.

[106] Singlehurst, *Sowing, Reaping, Keeping* (IVP, 2006), p. 38.

To ponder:

What is God's name and what does it mean to you?

Are there other names for God that are significant for you?

How do you feel about discussing what you believe about God with other people?

What aspects of who God is do you think you need to explore more deeply?

What do you think of the idea that Christian beliefs about God's identity exclude other understandings of god?

Appointer

The Lord God appointed a bush, and made it come up over Jonah, to give shade over his head, to save him from his discomfort; so Jonah was very happy about the bush. But when dawn came up the next day, God appointed a worm that attacked the bush, so that it withered. (Jonah 4:6-7)

In the translation that we used in our small group discussions these verses read slightly differently to the translation above. Rather than God "appointing" a bush and worm, they were both "provided" by God. The same variation occurred early in the story when God appointed/provided a fish and a little later when God provided/appointed the east wind. The same, fairly rare, Hebrew word, *manah*, is found in all four verses. Literally it means "to weigh out", and carries the idea of something being set up officially, counted out, prepared for, or appointed.[107]

We've already discussed the fish at some length, so in

---

[107] mânâh, maw-naw'; a prim. root; prop. to weigh out; by impl. to allot or constitute officially; also to enumerate or enroll:— appoint, count, number, prepare, set, tell. Strong, *The New Strong's Dictionary of Hebrew and Greek Words* (Nelson, 1996).

this section we're going to think about the other three things that the Lord appoints as provision for Jonah. We're going to consider what they might show us about God, and what their implications for mission might be.

The first of the three things that God appoints is a bush. Exactly what kind of bush this was is a question that has led to much speculation among commentators, and nobody is really sure. What is apparent, however, is that it grew quickly and provided welcome shade for Jonah as he sat on the hillside above Nineveh and sulked. At first glance this appointment seems to be in line with much of the familiar teaching about God's provision of shelter and care for God's people. It calls to mind the Psalmists' poetry of God's sheltering wings[108], echoed by Jesus as he looked over Jerusalem.[109] A second, deeper look, however, reveals something else. God's primary purpose in appointing the bush for Jonah was not to provide him with shade. It was to teach him an object lesson by depriving him of the shade that had been provided. We will think about what this might show

[108] e.g. Psalm 17:8,
[109] Luke 13:34

us of God's character when we consider the east wind, but for now we could reflect on whether Jonah might have been wise to have been suspicious of the speed with which the bush grew.

Sometimes in ministry things spring up quickly, and this makes us feel good. Without becoming cynical, it is perhaps sensible to maintain a level head when this happens. We can be thankful to God for the growth, whilst waiting for any long-term fruit to become apparent. We have already touched a couple of times on Jesus' story of the sower and the seeds that land in different types of ground. In this story Jesus describes one of the sets of seeds as "springing up quickly".[110] This seed is not the fruitful seed. It is the seed that has landed in rocky parts and has no depth of soil to draw on. In the end it fades as quickly as it sprang up.

The second thing that the Lord appointed was a worm. Adrian Plass tells the story of a fictional vicar who has a very poor relationship with the organist of the church. At one point the organist tells the choir that he has found a verse in the Old Testament that prophesies the arrival of this vicar at the church: "The

[110] Mark 4:5

Lord appointed a worm." (Jonah 4:7) This episode is related to the vicar by a "concerned" member of the choir. The vicar shares with his friends how he does indeed feel like a worm, weak and wriggly, when he considers this mistle-thrush of an organist.[111]

We may have heard many times that God's power is made perfect in weakness,[112] and we might even believe it, but there are different types of weakness and some of them are easier to embrace than others. The first type is the weakness of the worm that is appointed to do something that is entirely natural to it, but that has an effect that is much greater than it could have achieved alone. Alone, the worm is too weak to drive a man to despair. The worm, doing what it has been appointed to do, in line with God's purposes, has the power to do so. This is the kind of weakness that it is easier to embrace. We know that we have limited resources, but we trust that if we use them faithfully, in line with God's purposes, then we will see greater things happen than we could ever have imagined.

---

[111] Plass, *An Alien at St Wilfrid's* (Fount, 1992), p. 46-47.
[112] 2 Corinthians 12:9

The second type of weakness is much more uncomfortable. It is the weakness of the worm in the thrall of a thrush. It is the weakness that has no resources, but depends entirely on something other than itself for survival and, beyond that, for flourishing. In Plass' story the vicar is encouraged by his friends to invite the organist for a meal and be honest about the way that he is feeling about their relationship. This sort of radical honesty, confession and forgiveness can only be done with the grace of God and often with the help of friends. This kind of weakness is much more difficult to embrace, as it requires us to lay aside our pride and self-reliance entirely and to lean much more heavily into God's everlasting arms.[113]

As I walk around our estate I often feel like a worm. There is so much do to, and so many people to reach, and I am so small. I do have some resources, and I believe that God will magnify their impact as I apply them in line with God's purposes. However, I also believe that it is the way in which I treat those who make me feel like a worm that will be of the greatest

[113] David Crowder Band's cover of "Leaning on the Everlasting Arms" on their album "Give us Rest" has been a lifeline for us.

long-term significance.

The third thing that God appointed was a scorching east wind. To understand the impact of this provision, it is helpful to see it in its context. Jonah was angry at God for relenting. God provided a bush for shade and Jonah was happy. God removed the shade, and then made the conditions worse than they had been in the first place by sending the wind. Jonah's anger is deepened by despair. Having given Jonah new emotional experiences, God invites him to reconsider his attitude towards the Ninevites.

Discipline is not a popular concept, but the Bible is clear that followers of Jesus should expect to experience God's discipline. The writer of Hebrews[114] goes further in suggesting that the experience of being disciplined by God is one that assures us of our place in God's family and is a sign of God's love for us. And here we see what these appointments or provisions show us about what God is like. God is love, and loves us enough to discipline us. God loves others enough to cause us pain when we fail to love them as God does, in order that we might appreciate the depth of God's

[114] Hebrews 12:4-11

love for them. God will even destroy things that have previously been provided for our shelter, and to which we are very attached, if it is necessary for God's purposes in our lives and the lives of others.

This has two important implications for mission. The first is to do with how we approach difficulties, frustrations, hardship, and suffering as we engage in mission. We need to be aware of the possibility that God may be disciplining us. This may be a positive discipline, where we are being trained and strengthened for the work that we have been given to do. It may be a negative discipline, in which we are being invited to reconsider our attitudes or actions. Either way, we should take the possibility of God's discipline seriously and ask the Holy Spirit to make this clear to us.

The second is to do with how we talk to people about the Christian life. When we encourage people to follow Jesus it is important that we are honest with them about the cost of following Jesus, and about the reality of the demands that God makes on us.[115] Jesus

[115] God's chisel forms us into a masterpiece - http://www.youtube.com/watch?v=3QCkBL2DfVg

makes this clear in some teaching that was recorded by Luke.[116] Jesus tells his disciples that he expects them to give up everything to follow him. He suggests that it would be wise for people to consider this cost before making a decision about following him. If we are going to invite people to make this decision, it is our duty to give them all the information that we have.

To ponder:

Are there times in your life when you have been aware of God providing you with shelter?

What do you think about scepticism towards quickly-sprouting growth? Can it lead to a lack of faith in God's power to break through?

In what situations do you feel weakest?

How do you react when someone makes you feel like a worm?

Are you aware of having experienced God's discipline?

---

[116] Luke 14:25-33

Sovereign

But the Lord hurled a great wind upon the sea, and such a mighty storm came upon the sea that the ship threatened to break up. (Jonah 1:4)

Are they the Falkland Islands or the Malvinas Islands? This morning there was an open letter from the president of Argentina to the Prime Minister of Great Britain published in British newspapers.[117] This letter was the latest round in an ongoing dispute about sovereignty - an argument about who has the right to rule over, to make laws for, and to have taxes paid from, these islands in the Atlantic. Both nations have their own account of the history of the islands to justify their own claims. It seems that the people currently living there want to remain under British sovereignty, a desire that is due to be measured in a referendum.

God's sovereignty does have some similarities with national sovereignty - it has to do with who has the right to rule, to set laws, and to receive dues – but it

[117] http://www.guardian.co.uk/uk/2013/jan/02/cristina-fernandez-kirchner-letter-cameron

also has important differences. Unlike human sovereigns, God's sovereignty is absolute and does not depend upon anybody or anything else. The only king who has ever had the divine right to be king is God.

In the story of Jonah, God's sovereignty is displayed in various ways. God's sovereignty over humanity can be seen in God's pronouncement of judgement on Nineveh. It has been a place of wickedness that has broken God's sovereign law and God exercises a sovereign's right and duty to judge. God displays the sovereign right to relent when Nineveh repents. God's sovereignty over creation is revealed in the hurling of wind and storm on the sea. God has both the power to control nature's forces and the authority to direct them against Jonah and the boat that he was travelling in. This sovereignty is seen in the appointments that God made, which we discussed earlier. This sovereignty is seen in the success of the mission to the Ninevites, despite the attitude and methodology of Jonah.

This theme of sovereignty has two important things to say to our understanding of mission – the first about fear, the second about creativity.

The first observation is that a natural human reaction to the exercise of God's sovereignty is fear, and that this fear can be an important step on the road to repentance. The sailors feared and worshipped. The Ninevites feared and repented. Jonah says that he fears, but his conversation with God shows more anger than fear, and he ends up far from God.

This observation might lead us to consider what place the fear of God has in our understanding of mission. As we think about this, there are at least three aspects that need to be taken into account.

The first aspect is the repeated pattern of God, or God's messengers, telling people not to be afraid of God's immediate presence. This pattern first emerges in God's conversation with the man that God had chosen to be the ancestor of God's people. It is so early in their relationship that he is still called Abram, rather than Abraham. God appears to him in a vision and tells him not to be afraid, and reinforces the promise to him that he will have a son.[118] Throughout the Old Testament, God says "do not be afraid," when appearing to others including Hagar, Isaac, Jacob, and

[118] Genesis 15:1-5

Gideon. [119] This pattern continues into the New Testament, when the heralds of Jesus' arrival on earth appear to Mary and to the Shepherds and begin their messages by reassuring them.[120] Jesus himself stills his friends' fear when he appears to them following his resurrection, [121] and he continues with this ministry from his throne in heaven, as we hear in John's vision of heaven in Revelation.[122]

The second aspect is one that sees the fear of God as a good thing, and its absence as a problem. Abram's name is changed to Abraham, and the promise that God made to him is fulfilled. He has a son in his old age, a son called Isaac. God tests his faith by commanding him to sacrifice Isaac, but then calls a halt as Abraham raises the knife saying, "Now I know that you fear God."[123] Throughout the law-giving books of the Old Testament, the command is given to fear God and to obey the other commands because of

[119] Genesis 21:17, Genesis 26:24, Genesis 46:3, Judges 6:23
[120] Luke 1:30, Luke 2:10
[121] Luke 24:36
[122] Revelation 1:17
[123] Genesis 22:12

the fear of God.[124] This pattern continues into the New Testament where Jesus implies that the lack of a fear of God is wicked,[125] and Peter, in his second letter, repeats the command to fear God as part of the obedient life of faith.[126] Finally, in Revelation, we hear the call to fear God.[127]

The third aspect is the fact that, as we have seen in Jonah, the exercise of God's sovereignty may engender fear in people, and this can bring them closer to God. We see this happening on a few occasions in Jesus' time on earth. Right at the beginning of his ministry he was on another boat. He'd borrowed it from a fisherman called Peter to use as a waterborne speaking platform at the lake's edge.

When he finishes speaking he suggests that they go fishing. Peter's against it, because he's been out all night and caught nothing and knows full well that you don't catch anything on Galilee in the day; all the fish are hiding from the sun at the bottom of the lake.

[124] e.g. Deuteronomy 10:12
[125] Luke 18:2
[126] 1 Peter 2:17
[127] Revelation 14:7

Muttering under his breath, he pulls out from the shore and throws the nets over the side. Before he knows it the boat is starting to sink because there are so many fish in the nets. He lands the catch with the help of some friends and then falls on his knees and says to Jesus, "Go away from me Lord; I am a sinful man."[128] An encounter with God's sovereignty has made him afraid, and that fear will bring him closer to God.

Knowing how we reconcile these different aspects is still a work in progress for me. Here are some tentative suggestions. Firstly: it is not our job to make people afraid. Sometimes God will do this, but it is not our job. This suggestion is linked to the earlier discussion about repentance and Amos Starkadder. Secondly, it is our job to love people in a way that casts out fear.[129] People may be afraid for all kinds of reasons, including an encounter with the sovereignty of God. Whyever they are afraid, we know that an encounter with God's love can wipe away that fear. This is good news, and we should share it. Thirdly, it would be wise of us to maintain a healthy fear of God

[128] Luke 5:8, NIV
[129] 1 John 4:18

for ourselves.

Once we've considered what God's sovereignty means for our understanding of fear, we must also observe that God's sovereign playbook is much bigger than ours. Not only is it bigger, but it is more creative, containing moves that we could never pull off and even some that we just don't understand.

I moved to Stoke just in time for Stoke City's first season in the Premiership. I think it is fair to say that they have defied most people's expectations by not only surviving there but becoming a fairly solid mid-table team, with the occasional cup run and European adventure. They are known as a well-organised team; no massive stars on big wages, but honest, hard-working, competent players in a system that they understand with plans which they implement well. You can go a long way like that, but probably not to the top. To get to the top you need a player who seems to operate on a different level, who can see space that no-one else sees and can make the ball do the impossible - a Messi, a Ronaldo, a Pele.

In mission it is very tempting to become a well-organised team with a plan that we understand and which we implement well. We'll have read the latest on contextual mission, and we'll have been to the Fresh Expressions conference and taken note of what the speakers have said. We'll have listened to our context and to God and we'll have sorted out our Mission Action Plan. The reality is, however, that Jonah did none of these things. Jonah's methodology did not include spending time getting to know the community. He did not do any listening to the people. He didn't have much of a plan. Yet the whole city repented, by a sovereign work of God.

Our mission thinking, methods, tactics, and strategies are all good and worthwhile, but if they have no flexibility for God's sovereign creativity to blow through, they are not fit for purpose. Actually, if they don't depend on God's sovereign creativity to do something outrageous in order for them to come off, they are not fit for purpose. As Frog Orr-Ewing put it, "it's not meant to be doable."[130]

[130] Talk at Lichfield Diocesan Renewal Day 2012.

To ponder:

What place does fear have in your emotions about God?

How could you express the love that casts out fear?

How would you reconcile the different aspects on fear that appear in the Bible?

In what ways is the fear of the Lord the beginning of wisdom?

How does it feel to depend on God's sovereign action for your hopes and plans to bear fruit?

Pursuer

For the men knew that he was fleeing from the presence
of the Lord, because he had told them so. (Jonah 1:10b)

Unforgiven. The Thirty-Nine steps. Bullitt. The Fugitive. Catch Me If You Can. These are all great films built around the theme of pursuit. None of them, however, can come close to the pinnacle of this art form. I am, of course, referring to Droopy Dog in "Dumb Hounded". Our diminutive hero is relentless in his pursuit of the escaped convict wolf, able to predict and foresee his quarry's every move.

There is a sense in which we can read the book of Jonah as a story about God's pursuit of Jonah's heart. We know that Jonah was fleeing from God's presence, and we have seen how God acts sovereignly in different ways to make God's presence felt in the different situations that Jonah faces. This is done in order to bring him to a clearer knowledge of who God is, and of the depth and spread of God's love. We know that when we leave Jonah, he feels like he has been cornered by God, but he has not yet surrendered. And so the pursuit continues.

When we reflect on our pursuit of God, and on our vain attempts to elude God's presence, there are two themes that run through the Bible and Christian writings that can guide our thinking.

The first theme is that of omnipresence: God being everywhere at the same time. We get hints of this in Jonah, but it is more fully expressed by the Psalmist, who describes how God is inside, outside, before, after, above, below, east, west, in the dark and in the light.[131] God encompasses all that is. We have already spent some time thinking about the fact that God is always there first, and the implications of this fact for our missional thinking. We turn now, then, to consider a second theme, one that seems paradoxical given God's presence everywhere, but which is present in Scripture and therefore needs attention. It is the idea that God chases us.

In Luke's account of Jesus' life he shares two stories that Jesus told about people who had lost things, and their search for them.[132] He tells of a shepherd who has a hundred sheep. One of the sheep goes missing,

[131] Psalm 139
[132] Luke 15:1-10

so he leaves the other ninety-nine and goes hunting for the one that is lost. When he finds it, he brings it home, and invites his neighbours to celebrate with him. The second story is about a woman who loses a silver coin, probably part of her dowry. She spares no effort in getting light into the house and sweeping the corners until she finds it. Then, she also invites her neighbours to come and celebrate with her. Two people who lost something valuable. Two people who invested time and effort in finding what was lost. Two people who celebrated the finding of the lost.

What is really interesting is who Jesus told these stories to. Jesus was spending time with the wrong sort of people: whores and collaborators. The religious leaders were muttering into their beards about the bad company Jesus was keeping, and that's when he told them these stories. Amongst other things, when he tells these stories Jesus is making it clear to them that he is going to go out looking for those who are lost. He repeats this lesson even more explicitly on another occasion, when the upstanding citizens of a town are appalled at his decision to invite himself to eat with the local tax-collector, a man named Zacchaeus. Jesus says to them "the Son of Man came to seek and to save what was lost."[133]

Jesus saw his mission on earth as part of God's relentless pursuit. He came on a search-and-rescue mission. This search was so relentless that it would take him to the cross, through death and hell, and out the other side. Jesus pursues us so relentlessly that even death can't stop him. He is after us all.

Perhaps one of the most well-known explorations of this theme is found in "The Hound of Heaven", a poem written by Francis Thompson.[134] In it he explores some of the ways in which people try to evade God, and God's ever-faithful pursuit of them. Attempts to hide from God in time, in space, in nature, in pleasure, in sleep, are shown to be pointless: for none of them is beyond God's reach.

> Still with unhurrying chase,
> And unperturbéd pace,
> Deliberate speed, majestic instancy,
> Came on the following Feet,

[133] Luke 19:1-10

[134] http://en.wikisource.org/wiki/Hound_of_Heaven Read beautifully by Richard Burton here:
http://www.youtube.com/watch?v=gToj6SLWz8Q

And a Voice above their beat—
'Naught shelters thee, who wilt not shelter Me.'

Having shared what it feels like to be chased down by God, the poem ends at the moment of surrender when the spirit realises that all that it thought it was seeking is to be found in the one from whom it was running.

Is my gloom, after all,
Shade of His hand, outstretched caressingly?
'Ah, fondest, blindest, weakest,
I am He Whom thou seekest!
Thou dravest love from thee, who dravest Me.'

Thompson graphically captures the relentless nature of the pursuit that Jesus reveals in his stories of the lost sheep and the lost coin. When we comprehend this, I wonder what it might say about our mission priorities.

The first thing that occurs to me is to do with our own persistence, perseverance and doggedness. I believe that understanding the nature of God's pursuing constancy can encourage us in our own ministry to endure, and to keep searching. The temptation to discouragement in pioneer ministry can be severe. It can feel like two steps forward and one back. When we've been praying for somebody for months, and it seems to make no difference; when they still don't respond positively to our gentle invitations to explore faith, or to come and see; when somebody who we have been encouraging in their walk of discipleship falls or fails; when relationships in a new community take time to develop, or suddenly come crashing down around our ears because of one careless word or moment of forgetfulness. It is at these points that we can remember that God has never given up pursuing us and what is good for us, or pursuing those we have been called to serve, and what is good for them. And so, in faith and by grace, we also can persist in pursuit.

The second thing that occurs to me is in relation to priorities. Jesus talked of a shepherd who left ninety-nine and went to search for one. Some commentators assert that this is a joke; that Jesus is using hyperbole to make a point. No sensible shepherd, surely, would risk leaving ninety-nine sheep to find one that had wandered off. When I suggested this to a group of goat owners in South Sudan they rejected it. They were clear that each animal is valuable and that the good shepherd would make sure the ninety-nine were safe and go searching for the one. In most of our churches we do not have ninety-nine. We seem to have ended up in the reverse situation to the one that Jesus described. We have one sheep in the fold and ninety-nine are lost. It seems to me that we need to think very carefully about what this means for how we should use our time and energy. At the very least, we need to remember the most important number. The most important number is not the number of people in church on a Sunday, or who come to our activities, or who we have contact with. The important number is the population of the place that we are called to serve. On our estate there are 4,500 people. That is the important number. I am glad that of the 1,800 houses here I know of 50 which have church-going people living in them. I am challenged by the fact that there are 1,750 which don't. There are ninety-nine sheep lost on the hills of Priorslee, and God is after them.

The fact that it is God that is after them is massively reassuring. It is God, who is everywhere, so there is no-one so far from God that they can't be reached. We might not be able to see the way, but there is one.

There is no people group, no sub-culture, no language that is beyond God's pursuit.

The paradox that exists when we talk about an omnipresent God who pursues people is addressed in a conversation that is reported in the introduction of an edition of "The Hound of Heaven", between an examining professor and a student.[135]

'Well, what on earth does Thompson mean by that Hound?'

'He means God.'

'But is not that a rather irreverent way for Thompson to be talking about God, calling Him a hound? What does he mean by comparing God to a hound?'

'Well, he means the pursuit of God.'

'Oh, I see, Thompson is pursuing God, is he?'

'Oh, no. He is rather running away from God.'

[135] http://www.gutenberg.org/files/30730/30730-h/30730-h.htm

Well, then, God is pursuing Thompson, is that it?'

'Yes, that's it.'

'But, see here; according to Thompson's belief God is everywhere, isn't He?'

'Yes.'

'Well, then, how can God be going after Thompson? Is it a physical pursuit?'

'No. It is a moral pursuit.'

'A moral pursuit! What's that? What is God after?'

'He is after Thompson's love.'

God was after Thompson's love. God was after Jonah's love. God is after your love, and mine. God is after every love, and God calls us to join the chase.

To ponder:

Can you remember a time when it felt like you were being pursued?

How did it feel?

Do you see your journey to faith as a pursuit?

What do you think about describing your mission as pursuing others?

What encourages you to keep going to the face of difficulties and challenges?

What is the most important number in the context that God has sent you to serve?

Conversion

When God saw what they did, how they turned from their evil ways, God changed his mind about the calamity that he had said he would bring upon them; and he did not do it. (Jonah 3:10)

Now, this is a bit embarrassing. I've just spent the last section going on about how God is relentless, unwavering, immovable. And now, here we have God's mind being changed, God repenting and not doing what had been said. Fortunately for me, there is a clue to the resolution of this embarrassment just around the corner. Jonah, in his anger at God, says this: "I knew that you are a gracious God and merciful, slow to anger, and abounding in steadfast love, and ready to relent from punishing."[136]

Jonah, for all his faults, understands something about the unchangeable nature of God. He knows that God is open to a conversion of action and declared decision, because of a consistency in God's nature. God's change of mind is entirely consistent with, and in fact demonstrates, God's consistent nature. God is

---

[136] Jonah 4:2

consistently full of grace, willing to show mercy, and loving. Because this nature is reliable and sure, unchanging and dependable, God is free to change decisions and actions. If this were not the case, if God were bound by what had been said to people, despite changes in circumstances and attitudes to God, then the character of God would have to be different.

One of the things that I find most difficult is changing my mind. This is true in a whole collection of different contexts. When my children have asked if they can do something and I've said no, they may be able to explain why it's a good idea, my wife might have a quiet word about why she thinks it would be fine, they might even tidy their rooms. Still, I find it difficult to change my mind. When I've decided what would be a good idea for an outreach activity, I feel for the person that asks the difficult, probing, searching, tempering questions about it. I've had an idea, and I like it, and will defend it to the bitter end.

None of the things that make it difficult for me to change my mind - pride, desire for control, standing on authority - none of them are Godly or good. This difficulty I have reveals something about my nature - something that is immovable and persistent, but not in a good way. One might even call it obstinacy. If we had a God who always acted in accordance with announced decisions, rather than in accordance with constant love, then there would be no grace, no cross, and no redemption.

One of the best explanations of how this works is given by God to the prophet Jeremiah. God sends Jeremiah to see the local potter. Whilst he's there, he sees that the potter is making a pot on a wheel. As Jeremiah watches, the potter decides that the pot that he is making has gone wrong, it is spoilt. So, the potter changes his mind about what he's making and makes something else, a different shaped pot, from the same piece of clay. Jeremiah then hears God speaking to him again:

> *If at any time I announce that a nation or kingdom is to be uprooted, torn down and destroyed, and if that nation I warned repents of its evil, then I will relent and not inflict on it the disaster I had planned.* (Jeremiah 18:7-8, NIV)

God explains clearly to Jeremiah exactly what we have

seen work out in Nineveh. God may declare what seems to be an absolute judgement, but there is always an implicit contingency. It may not be spoken aloud, but it is taken as read. If the person or people under judgement repent, then God will relent. It doesn't have to be said every time; it is understood. Jonah understood. The people of Nineveh hoped that it might be true for them. By the grace of God, it was. This is the kind of Godly change of mind that we are comfortable with, that reassures us and is relatively easy to understand and accept.

What is more difficult to accept, and is distinctly less comforting, is what God says to Jeremiah next:

> *And if at another time I announce that a nation or kingdom is to be built up and planted, and if it does evil in my sight and does not obey me, then I will reconsider the good I had intended to do for it.* (Jeremiah 18:9-10, NIV)

It may be less comfortable, but it has its roots in the same soil. God's decisions and intentions are subject to change because God's character is constant. God is holy and just, righteous and pure. If people begin to take God's blessing and favour for granted, and begin to do wrong, then God is at liberty to withdraw that blessing and favour. This is because God is love. God loves completely. God loves us too much to continue blessing us indefinitely while we walk away from him. God loves us too much to continue blessing indefinitely those who are a curse to others.

I think it is also possible to see this second sense of God's change of mind illustrated in Jonah. Jonah, as an individual, is shaken up by all he's been through. His prejudices and hatreds are challenged by God. As such, he is a representative of his people, the people of God. His failure to love and be compassionate is shared widely amongst the people of God, and God is warning the people: I have chosen you and announced that you are to be built up and planted. However, you are lacking in love and compassion. This is disobedience. Remember that I am a God who repents. I will remind you of this by forgiving Nineveh, despite the fact that I said that I would destroy the city. Remember that I can also change my mind about the future I have promised you, if you do not obey me.

When I first began thinking about looking for jobs after my curacy, I went to Glasshampton Monastery with my wife. We spent the day praying and listening to God. We took some notes about some of the things that we believed that God was saying to us. Some of them seemed to be applicable to the work in Priorslee, and those matches made up part of the decision to apply for this role. Since then we have continued to pray and to listen, with others, for Priorslee. We have kept a record of the words and pictures that have been shared with us. We have reflected on them, sifted them, and weighed them. At different times we have discerned different emphases in what God is calling us to. What has been constant, however, is the sense that despite the hardness of the ground and the challenges that exist, there will be fruit here. That there are green shoots, and that there can be a blossoming; that harvest time is coming. This has been, and continues to be, an encouragement to us to keep going when things are tough.

What Jonah and Jeremiah seem to be teaching us is that these words and encouragements from God are contingent. They are not absolute, but rather their fulfilment depends on obedience to God. In some senses this is obvious and incontrovertible. If I were to start drinking myself into a stupor every night at the local pub, beating my children, or having a string of affairs, it is not controversial to say that God's stated purposes for me and for Priorslee may be frustrated. In cases of catastrophic and flagrant moral failure, then it is easy to see how ministries and communities can be damaged and scarred in ways that take generations to heal.

What might be more worrying, however, is not the immediately disastrous but the chronically abrading; not the obvious, but the subtle. We may feel able to avoid rebellious disobedience, but be unsure that we are always ready to surrender in radical obedience. We may not hate, but we struggle to embrace love in all its depth and glory. Running unchecked, these worries might reduce the encouragement that we find in the promises of God, causing us to believe that they are contingent, and depend on our actions and faithfulness. Knowing ourselves, even a little, this feels like unsure ground.

And, of course, this is the point. We need to know that if we depend on ourselves, we *are* on unsure ground. It is when we know ourselves to be unsure that we learn to lean even more heavily on God, whose character and nature is sure. God is surely loving, thoroughly good, and wholly dependable. The danger comes when we believe ourselves to be firm, and become sure of ourselves. It is at this point that all is really at risk because we are tempted to stop looking to God, and to start working with our own strength. As Paul wrote to his friends in Corinth, "if you think you are standing, watch out that you do not fall."[137] However, by the sure grace of God we can avoid falling by taking to heart what Jesus says. "Blessed are the poor in spirit, for theirs is the kingdom of heaven."[138]

> **To ponder:**
>
> Do you find it easy or difficult to change your mind?
>
> What kind of things make it easier or more difficult?
>
> Have you experienced God's mind changing?
>
> What promises of God are most precious to you?
>
> How do you feel about the suggestion that those promises have an implicit contingency?
>
> In what areas of your life are you most vulnerable to worrying that you fall short of what God asks of you?
>
> What unchanging characteristic of God might bring peace to those worries?

[137] 1 Corinthians 10:12
[138] Matthew 5:3

God

Jesus

*For just as Jonah became a sign to the people of
Nineveh, so the Son of Man will be to this generation.*
(Luke 11:30)

God has a mission, and so Jonah went to Nineveh. God
has a mission, and so God, in Jesus, came to earth. God
has a mission, and so we go into the world. Whilst God
was here, physically with us, he compared the people
he was talking to with the people of Nineveh. He also
made a comparison between himself and Jonah. Both
Luke [139] and Matthew [140] record accounts of Jesus
saying to people that they would not receive a sign,
except the sign of Jonah. He didn't, however, say what
he meant by the sign of Jonah, and because Luke and
Matthew based what they wrote on slightly different
recollections of what had been said, there are a
variety of different suggestions.

Some suggest that the sign of Jonah was the message
of judgement that Jonah preached, which is echoed by
Jesus' preaching in his generation. Jonah preached

[139] Luke 11:29-32
[140] Matthew 12:39-41

201

that Nineveh was to be destroyed, and Jesus preached that the Kingdom of God was near, calling in people to repent. This possibility is given weight by the context in which Jesus was actually speaking, and to which he said that the current generation was evil and was resisting the call to repentance in a way that the people of Nineveh hadn't. On the other hand, it is not usual for preaching to be understood in the Bible as a sign. Signs tended to be miraculous acts of power and authority.

In light of this, others suggest that the sign of Jonah was his captivity in the fish's stomach and subsequent rescue. This is paralleled in Jesus' life by his death and resurrection. Both of these miraculous signs are seen as God's demonstration of the authority of the person sent to speak for God. This explanation is backed up by what Jesus says about it in Matthew's account. It also explains why the future tense is used; Jesus talks about the sign of Jonah as one that *will be* given. This does, however, assume that the people of Nineveh knew that Jonah had been in a fish, for which there is no evidence in the story. We are not told that the people of Nineveh repented because of the sign of Jonah emerging from the stomach of the fish, and believed him because of the authority he gained from this miraculous event. Rather they repented because of the message of judgement he brought. Similarly, there is no evidence that at the time the people who were listening to Jesus understood him to be talking about his future death and resurrection, and no evidence that they were more open to receiving his message because this sign was to come. It is also worth noting that Luke doesn't even mention this as a possibility.

A third suggestion is that the sign of Jonah was Jonah himself. Jonah's presence as the messenger of God in the city showed Nineveh that God existed and was concerned about what was going on there. It might be countered that Jonah's simple presence is no more a miraculous sign than his preaching, and that without his preaching his presence would have been pointless. In Jesus' case, however, his presence, as God on earth, is in itself miraculous. It also may not have been understood as such at the time, but nevertheless it is the case. There is also evidence that there were those who saw and understood this sign, and then believed because of it.

We cannot know exactly what Jesus meant when he

referred to the sign of Jonah. In some senses this does not matter a great deal. The important thing about any sign is not the form that it takes but what it points towards. Whether the sign of Jonah was what was preached, what miracles occurred, or who Jonah was, are all questions of form. What is important is that all of these forms point in the same direction. All three point to God, the God of mission. The signs of Jonah's message, his rescue from the fish, and his presence in Nineveh all pointed the people of Nineveh to God in a way that prompted them to repentance. This was despite the flaws in Jonah's words and attitude.

Jesus' message, his resurrection from death, and his presence on earth all point people to God. In contrast to Jonah, however, Jesus was a perfect sign who represented God perfectly, because he was and is God. His message is God's message; his words, God's words. He spoke with an authority that wasn't dependent on his power over nature and illness, but which flowed from who he is. His resurrection demonstrated that this power extends to power over death, a divine victory that was only achievable by the one who is not naturally subject to death, but who chose to become subject to it so that he could defeat it. Jesus' presence on earth was God's presence on earth, which now continues in the presence of the Holy Spirit, who was sent to empower and guide God's people as they walk in Jesus' way.

If this is true, and both Jonah and Jesus are signs that point towards God, what can we learn about God from the signs of Jonah and Jesus? I believe that from every angle Jonah signifies a God who is missionary. God is loving, merciful, and faithful. God is there before Jonah, paving the way, and God is there behind Jonah, sending him forward. God has a mission of outreach to those who are not the people of God. God has a mission of inreach to those who are already the people of God. God involves all people and all creation in those missions of outreach and inreach. God's mission is carried out in God's way, and that way is sometimes obscure to us and difficult to understand, but God carries it out with sovereign power and authority.

It would take another book (or more) to explore all that we can learn about our missionary God from the life of Jesus. There is, however, one story that Jesus told which I would like to conclude by focussing on. This story is recorded, with slight variations, by

Matthew, Mark, and Luke.

Jesus told of a man who had plans for a vineyard.[141] He spent time preparing the soil, clearing it of rocks, and protecting it with a wall and a watchtower. Once it was all ready, planted and fruitful, he gave it over to a group of farmers who rented it from him. At harvest time the owner of the vineyard sent a servant to claim his share of the crop. The tenant farmers beat him up. The owner sent another servant. They beat him up as well. The owner decided to send his son, believing that the tenants would not dare to attack him. The tenants, however, did dare. In fact, they convinced themselves that if they killed the son, then there would be no one to inherit and they would be able to keep the vineyard and all its harvest. So they murdered the son. The father of the son came and destroyed the tenants and gave the vineyard to others.

Jesus told this story against the religious leaders of the time. They understood that he had reshaped an ancient story of their faith[142] to make the point that they would be held accountable for the harvest of the

---

[141] Matthew 21:33-46, Mark 12:1-12, Luke 20:9-19
[142] Isaiah 5:2

fruitful land with which they had been entrusted. On the way Jesus makes another point. In this story the father and the son believed that the son would live. In reality both the Father and the Son knew that the Son would die. They were willing to go through the pain and grief of that experience because, in the end, the sign of Jonah, and of Jesus, comes down to this:

For God so loved the world that he gave his one and only Son, that whoever believes in him shall not perish but have eternal life. For God did not send his Son into the world to condemn the world, but to save the world through him.
(John 3:16-17, NIV)

Jesus said, "Peace be with you! As the Father has sent me, I am sending you."
(John 20:21, NIV)